SKETCH

of the

Twelfth Alabama Infantry

of

BATTLE'S BRIGADE, RODES' DIVISION,
EARLY'S CORPS,

of the

Army of Northern Virginia,

ROBERT EMORY PARK, of Macon, Georgia,
Late Captain Company F, 12th Alabama Regiment.

[Reprinted from *Southern Historical Society Historical Papers*, Vol. XXXIII.]

RICHMOND:
W. M. Ellis Jones, Book And Job Printer.
1906

Sketch of the Twelfth Alabama Infantry
By Captain Robert Emory Park

Edited by Frank B. Powell, III

©2022 The Scuppernong Press

First Printing

The Scuppernong Press
PO Box 1724
Wake Forest, NC 27588
www.scuppernongpress.com

Cover design by Gemma Bernard
Book design by Frank B. Powell, III

All rights reserved

Printed in the United States of America

No part of this book may be reproduced or transmitted in any form or by any means, electronic or mechanical, including photocopying, recording, or by any information and storage and retrieval system, without written permission from the editor and/or publisher.

International Standard Book Number ISBN 978-1-942806-49-3

Library of Congress Control Number: 2022949880

Contents

Prefatory Note v
Sketch of the Twelfth Alabama 1
Field and Staff 3
Captains and Counties from which the Companies Camp ..3
Twelfth Alabamians who surrendered at Appomattox 16
Twelfth Alabama Regiment..17
The Yorktown Election and Reorganization 18
The Battle of Williamsboro 22
Seven Pines...23
List of Killed and Wounded at Seven Pines 29
The Seven Days Battle Around Richmond....................33
Winter at Hamilton's Crossing...36
Battle of Chancellorsville..44
Advance into Maryland and Pennsylvania 47
Battle of Gettysburg..49
Camp Near Orange Courthouse, August 1863....................51
Battle of Warrenton Springs 54
Battle of Bristow Station 55
Battle of Locust Grove 59
Battle of Mine Run 59
At Washington City..70
Re-enlistment For the War..75
Anniversary of the Battle of Boonesboro, Maryland...........83
Battle of Winchester...85
The Twelfth's Artillery Associations............................92
Preaching in Camp..93
Major General R. E. Rodes 94
Music in the Camp..95
The Twelfth Alabama Surgeons 96
Battle of the Wilderness...97
The Twelfth of May...98

Captain Robert Emory Park

Prefatory Note.

This compilation toward a sketch of the history of this gallant regiment, its organization, associations, engagements, casualties, etc., consists of extracts from the *War Diary of Robert Emory Park*, late Captain of Company "F," with other materials contributed and collected by him.

A portion of the *War and Prison Diary* covering the period January 27. 1864, June 15, 1865, appeared as a serial in the *Southern Historical Society Papers*, Vols. I, II, III, (1876-7), at the request of the former Secretary of the Society, Rev. J. William Jones, D. D., who in prefatory note commends "its value in that it records the daily experience of the men who followed our distinguished leaders, and gives the impressions made upon the mind of an intelligent young soldier as he discharged his daily duty."

An earlier portion of the *Diary*, January, 1863, January 27. 1864, with account of the battles of Chancellorsville, Gettysburg, Warrenton, Bristow Station, Mine Run, the march into Maryland and Pennsylvania, and reminiscences of the battle of Seven Pines, etc., appeared in Vol. XXVI. Its preservation was fortuitous, having been lost on the field of battle. It was returned in a somewhat mutilated condition in 1888 by Mrs Vine Smith, of Lebanon, N. H., to Capt. Park.

The prime value of contemporaneous record is indisputable, but the ingenuous *Diary* of this devoted and conscientious young soldier is in its convincing verity as the instantaneous photograph of passing events.

Capt. Park has proven himself in maturer years as progressive, public-spirited and successful as a citizen as he was gallant and faithful as a soldier. He was called to the responsible trust of Treasurer of the State of Georgia in October, 1900, and will doubtless obtain it by general acclaim whilst he lives. The reverential spirit abides with him.

He is an active participant in the Reunions of Confederate Veterans, and in that held in Macon, Ga., Nov. 9th, 1905, his presence was signal in its inspiring influence.

He introduced a series of resolutions urging the Legislature of Georgia to make a liberal appropriation "as one of the original thirteen States" to be properly represented at the Tercentenary Celebration in May, 1907, of the first permanent settlement of the Anglo-Saxon race in America, at Jamestown. He witnessed also the laying of the cornerstone at Macon, Ga., of the first monument to the women of the South, who embody all of feminine virtue and blessing. He is also vice-president of the John B. Gordon Monument Association. Nor is the zeal of Mrs. Park to be less regarded. She is continuously re-elected the Regent for the State of Georgia of the Confederate Memorial Literary Society, whose inestimable treasures are preserved in what was the White House of the Confederacy in this city, the whilom residence of President Jefferson Davis.

Mrs. Park is the daughter of the late Dr. George R. and Cornelia (Paine) Hendree, formerly of Richmond, Virginia. Mrs. Hendree, who died at the residence of her daughter, Mrs. Park, January 6th, 1906, in the 84th year of her age, was the daughter of the late Edward Courtenay and Caroline Matilda (Brinton) Paine. The father a distinguished lawyer, born in Baltimore, Md., having moved to the South, impressed himself by his abilities in a long life, and was revered as the Nestor of the Georgia bar.

Mrs. Hendree was the mother of three daughters and an only son: Mrs. Park, Mrs. Georgia Hendree Burton, the wife of Right Rev'd Lewis William Burton, D. D., for years the beloved rector of the appealing St. John's Church, Richmond, Va., and the first Bishop of the Diocese, of Lexington, Ky., which was organized in January, 1896, and of Mrs. Harrison, the wife of Col. Z. D. Harrison, the Clerk of the Supreme Court of Georgia.

The son, Edward Paine Hendree, a gallant youth, fell at the age of 19 years in the sanguinary battle of the Wilderness, Va., May 5th, 1864, in the command of the company from Macon county, Ala., 61st Alabama Infantry, C. S. A.

It is to be hoped that the continuous efforts of Capt. Park will eventuate in the publication of a history of the 12th Alabama adequate to its deserts as so nobly attested.

R. A. BROCK, Editor.

Sketch of the Twelfth Alabama

While a student, in the last term of the Junior class, in what is now the Polytechnic College at Auburn, Ala., in May, 1861, I learned from my brother, Dr. J. F. Park of Tuskegee, that the last company which the Secretary of War would accept for a period of twelve months was being organized in that city. In response to this information I bade farewell to my college-mates and Professors and hurrying to Tuskegee, succeeded in having my name enrolled as one of the "Macon Confederates." A week afterward about a dozen more Auburn College boys joined the same company.

The officers of the company were, Hon. R. F. Ligon, State Senator, Captain, Prof. R. H. Keeling, First Lieut. Prof. W D. Zuber, Second Lieut., Captain George Jones, Third Lieut.

After going to Greenville, Ga., and bidding my mother and sisters good-bye, I joined the company at La Grange, as it passed there on its way to Richmond, reaching that city on the 10th of June. On the 12th day of June, 1861, the company was sworn into service for a period of twelve months. For several days the company was drilled regularly by our accomplished First Lieut., who was a graduate of the Virginia Military Institute, and who had served as Adjutant of the First Virginia Regiment during the Mexican War.

We were detained at Richmond waiting for other companies, with the expectation of forming a regiment of ten Alabama companies. During our stay we had a visit from President Davis, who rode into camp and witnessed our company drill. He expressed his approval of the company and was very gracious and courteous to the officers, who held a brief conversation with him.

Twelfth Alabama Infantry

Contributed to *"Brewer's Alabama,"* page 608, by Captain R. E. Park:

"The Twelfth Alabama was organized at Richmond in July, 1861, and at once moved to the Potomac front. It was first brigaded under General R. S. Ewell, of Virginia, who was soon after succeeded by General Rodes, of Alabama. The regiment reached Manassas on the 22nd of July, the day after the great battle, and after forming camp was detailed to bury the Federal dead. The Confederate dead had already been properly interred, but the fields and woods seemed to be full of the bodies of men in blue. My detail spent the day burying Brooklyn Zouaves, who wore blue jackets and red pantaloons. These Zouaves had been lying on the ground for several hours, and were greatly swollen, and their faces and hands had become black. The sight was a horrible one, and the removal of them to the long trenches which we dug, was anything but a grateful task, but it was a humane duty which we did not shrink from performing. We placed their heads looking towards the East, and were careful to bury them so deep that they would not be disturbed by predatory animals. This furious battle, and these terrible sights as a result, made an indelible impression upon us all. The regiment remained there during the fall and winter, and moved to Yorktown in the spring of 1862 It was under fare there and suffered lightly at Williamsburg. At Seven Pines the regiment was in the advance that opened the battle, and stormed the redoubt held by Casey's division, carrying three lines of works by successive charges, with the loss of 70 killed and 141 wounded — more than half of its number engaged. It participated, to some extent, in the other battles before Richmond, and mustered 120 men for duty after the battle of Malvern Hill. Still under Rodes, and in D. H. Hill's division, and brigaded with the Third, Fifth, Sixth and Twenty-Sixth Alabama Regiments, the Twelfth was in the advance into Maryland. It bore a conspicuous part at Boonsboro, and also at Sharpsburg, losing in these bloody conflicts 27 killed, 69 wounded, and 33 missing, out of its thinned ranks. Retiring into Virginia with the army, the regiment wintered on the Rappahannock. It was under fire but not actively engaged at Fredericksburg, but, it was in the resistless column of Rodes at Chancellorsville, where Colonel O'Neal led the brigade, and where the Twelfth charged three lines of breastworks, and was badly mutilated. It skirmished at Brandy Station, and again led the way over the Potomac. At Gettysburg it was on the extreme left and pressed the enemy in confusion through the town, then supported the grand assault and afterward covered the rear. After the army had retired into Virginia, the Twelfth was engaged in several skirmishes — at Warrenton Springs, Mine Run, etc. The winter was passed near Orange C. H., and the regiment — General Battle now commanded the brigade — was hotly engaged at the Wilderness and Spotsylvania, and in the continuous skirmishing of Grant's advance movement to Cold Harbor. The Twelfth again marched into Maryland when Early threatened Washington. It participated at Winchester with very severe loss, and in the further operations of the corps in the valley. On its return to Petersburg it took part — now in Gordon's corps — in the fierce struggles around that historic city, and laid down its arms at Appomattox. Of the original number of 1,196, about 50 were at Appomattox, and of the 321 recruits received, about 70 were there. Nearly 250 died of wounds received in battle, about 200 died of disease, and 202 were discharged. The battle flag of the Regiment is now in Mobile.

Field and Staff.

Colonel Robert T. Jones, of Perry, killed at Seven Pines.

Colonel B. B. Gayle, of Morgan, promoted from Captain; killed Boonsboro.

Colonel Samuel B. Pickens, of South Carolina, promoted from Adjutant; wounded at Spotsylvania and Winchester.

Lieutenant Colonel Theodora O'Hara, of Kentucky, the author of the world renowned lyric, *The Bivouac of the Dead*, and that almost as famous, *The Pioneer,* Buried in Frankfort, Ky.

Lieutenant Colonel }. C. Goodgame of Coosa Co.

Major E. D. Tracy, of Madison; transferred. Promoted Brigadier General. Killed at Grand Gulf, Miss. Brother of Major Philip Tracy of the 6th Georgia, who was killed at Gettysburg. Was a college classmate of Major John W Park of Greenville, Georgia, brother of Capt. R. E. Park.

Major John C. Brown of Coffee, resigned.

Major Adolph Proskauer, promoted from Captain, Company C, wounded at Chancellorsville and Spotsylvania.

Adjutant S. B. Pickens of South Carolina.

Adjutant L. Gayle of Virginia.

Captains and Counties from which the Companies Came.

The commissioned officers of the different Companies, as I can now recall them, and after diligent inquiry of survivors of the various companies that I have been able to reach by letter, were as follows:

Company A, "Guard Lafayette," Mobile, Ala.

Captain G. Heuilly, resigned June, 1862, died in Mobile, Ala., about the close of the war.

Company C.

Jules L'Etondal, resigned the latter part of 1862 on account of ill-health, died in Mobile, Ala., in 1865.

F. A. Rogers, died since war in New Orleans.

First Lieutenants: Jules L'Etondal, F. A. Rogers. John R. Williams, promoted first lieutenant May, 1862, surrendered with the army at Appomattox, now living in Mobile, Ala., an honored citizen and harbor master.

Second Lieutenant E. Lambert, reported as deserter.

Second Lieutenant Olivia Eugene, resigned June, 1862. No record.

Second Lieutenant J. B. Conche, resigned June, 1862. No further record.

This company left Mobile for the front in June, 1862. From it the following members were killed:

Sergeant N. Leonard, June 22, 1862, at Cold Harbor.
Corporal Alexander Porter, at Boonsboro.
James Kearns, at Spotsylvania, May 11, 1864.
Thomas Bennett, in skirmish near Richmond, June 28, 1864.
Louis Earnest, at Gettysburg.
Charles Rominger, at Seven Pines.
William Carroll, at Sharpsburg.
S. Logue, at Seven Pines.
James Campbell, at Sharpsburg.
Louis Dendarro, at Wilderness.
A. Brickhart, at Spotsylvania.
Ben Hammond, at Sharpsburg.
S. Stansell, at the Wilderness.
J. A. Jones, at Charlestown, Va.
C. Lanier, at Seven Pines.
J. B. McElroy, at Winchester.
J. Nugent, at Chancellorsville.
C. Frisbie, at Sharpsburg.
John Canau, at Wilderness.
H. W Robertson, at Sharpsburg.
B. Reily, at Gettysburg.
John Camuy, at Boonsboro.
William Muldoon, at Spotsylvania.

The following parties connected with this fine company should be recorded:

Sergeant W M. Wilson. Was transferred to the navy in 1861, and died in Mobile, Ala., in 1882.

Corporal E. Pettit. Was transferred and killed in Tennessee in 1863.

John Perry. Transferred to navy in 1862, and was with Admiral Semmes on the *Alabama* in the sea fight with *Kearsage*.

J. A. McCreary. Surrendered with the army at Appomattox, and joined the United States army after the war and was killed on Plains.

I would add the following names as having been transferred from this company to the Confederate navy:

Angelo Eldridge. Died in Mobile September 20, 1902.

Edward Martin. Died in Mobile in 1887.

Thomas Hansel.

Thomas Martin. Died in Mobile in 1888.

Company B "Coosa Independents" — Coosa County.

Captain J. H. Bradford was quite an old man, more than sixty years of age, wholly unacquainted with the duties of a Drill Master or of a Captain and soon resigned.

Captain John C. Goodgame, promoted from Orderly Sergt. to Captain, thence to Major and Lieut. Col. This gallant officer was killed after the War at Athens, Texas, being assassinated in his own house through an open window. He was Sheriff of his county.

Captain Henry W Cox, promoted from First Lieut., killed at Chancellorsville.

Captain Pat Thomas, promoted from First Lieut., killed at Appomattox.

First Lieut. Thomas Marbury, promoted from Second Lieut. Obtained a substitute and resigned, but with his resignation in his pocket, he went into the battle of Chancellorsville, and fought gallantly through it, escaping unwounded.

Second Lieutenants; Wm. Leonard.

Company C "Independent Rifles" — Mobile County.

Captain Stikes, resigned.

Captain Fred C. Fisher, an excellent scholar and fine officer, who served until nearly the close of the war, since which, having inherited a considerable fortune in Germany, he removed to Hamburg where he now resides, unmarried.

Captain Adolph Proskauer, promoted to Major. An interesting circumstance connected with Major Proskauer is that he was a German Jew, of excellent education, very handsome personal appearance, and perhaps the best dressed man in the regiment. He became Senior Captain, and while we were encamped near Fredericksburg in 1863, there being a vacancy in the position of Major of the regiment, he made formal application for promotion. Col. Pickens did not favor his appointment but preferred Capt. John W McNeely, of Company F, who was an able young officer and former teacher at Tuskegee and at Auburn, Alabama, and who was thoroughly equipped for the position of Major, and was second in rank.

In order to carry out his wishes the Colonel obtained the appointment of an Examining Court of the most distinguished character, namely, Gen. Junius Daniel, Gen. S. D. Ramseur, both of N. C. Brigades, and Col. E. L. Hobson of the 5th Ala. It was stated in camp that Col. Pickens hinted to this Committee of Examiners that he hoped they would be so rigid that Capt. Proskauer could not pass the examination.

During the day of the examination there was unusual interest felt by the officers of the camp, and especially by the Colonel. Late in the afternoon, after an all-day examination had been concluded, one of the officers rode rapidly up to Col. Pickens' headquarters and in reply to an anxious inquiry, was told that the committee had done all they could to defeat Capt. Proskauer, but that after an examination squad drill, in company drill, in regimental drill, in brigade drill, in drill by echelon, and in the army movements as suggested in Jomini's tactics, Captain Proskauer did not fail to answer promptly and accurately every question. The General added, "he knows more about tactics than any of the Examining Committee, and we were forced to recommend his promotion."

I recall seeing this gallant officer at the battle of Gettysburg, calmly standing amid his regiment, smoking a cigar, issuing his orders and animating the men, until a bullet though his cheek disabled him, and he became a prisoner of war.

Major Proskauer was a prominent citizen of Mobile after the war, represented Albania as a Democrat in the Legislature, was president of the Hebrew congregation of his city, and in 1895 he moved to St. Louis, Mo., where he soon became a prominent business man and highly esteemed citizen, becoming president of a Hebrew congregation in that city, and maintaining a reputation as a man of culture, refinement, integrity and rare business capacity He died in 1900 greatly lamented.

Company C.

First Lieutenant A. Scheuerman.

Second Lieutenant E. Karcher. Lieutenant Karcher was a native of Germany and was a Jew. He was a gallant soldier, and after the war became Lieutenant of Police of Mobile, Ala., where he died, esteemed as an excellent citizen, only a few years ago.

Second Lieutenants A. Eichom, F : Mumme.

Company D, " Coffee Rangers" — Coffee County.

Captain John Canty Brown, promoted to major; resigned; died in Florida.

Captain Exon Tucker; killed at Sharpsburg.

Captain James T. Davis; killed at Gettysburg. This last brave officer, with his company, was resting by a fence as we approached Gettysburg, and under heavy fire of the enemy's artillery, when a cannon ball ricocheted, struck him in the head and instantly translated him to a better world. His brains spattered over me and my companions near by, and the experience was a most distressing one.

Company E.

Captain R. W Higgins. This officer lived at Larkinsville, Ala., where he practiced law, and died soon after his resignation of his command. He died of consumption in November, 1861.

Captain L. D. Patterson. He was elected from private by unanimous vote of the company, and commanded it until April, 1862, when he was elected lieutenant colonel of the regiment and immediately resigned his commission and returned to Alabama. He was a teacher of fine reputation. He died on the 20th December, 1885.

Captain William L. Meroney. He was promoted to succeed Captain Patterson, and resigned one year later and returned to Alabama and resumed his practice as a physician. He died in Comanche, Tex., in 1904.

Captain Philip A. Brandon, of Chattanooga, Tenn., a very intelligent and faithful member of this company, has written an excellent pamphlet called the *Muster Roll of Company E, 12th Alabama Regiment*, and it is a souvenir of great interest and value, and should be in the hands, not only of every member of Company E, but of the 12th Alabama.

Captain C. M. Thomason. He succeeded Captain Meroney, but resigned his commission and joined the Seventh Alabama cavalry. He was a teacher of note.

Captain John Rogers was promoted captain of the company, and on May 12, 1864, while leading a charge at Spotsylvania Courthouse, was mortally wounded, and on the 19th of the month died. He was a gallant young man.

First Lieutenants: W. L. Meroney, C. M. Thomason, John Rogers.

Second Lieutenants R. H. McCampbell, W. A. Lankford, Alex. Majors. Of this officer I have written in connection with the battle of Snicker's Gap, where he was killed by my side.

Casualties.

At the battle of Seven Pines, May 31, 1862, twelve of this fine company were killed on the field, namely:

C. C. Bartles, Joel Coffey, J. C. Cunningham, W H. Crow, William Fields, Joseph Moore, F. M. Merrell, F. P. Patterson, A. G. Roberts, William Taylor, James Hudson and W. W. Hartman.

Thirty-five (35) others of the company, were wounded but recovered. Fifty-six (56) of the company were in this battle. There were 101 members in the company originally.

The following were killed in various battles of the war:

J. E. Estes, at the Wilderness.

C. H. Hunter and N. B. Rucks, at Chancellorsville.

W. T. Keaton, at Winchester, Va.

Jacob Mitchell and J. A. Mikles, at Boonsboro, Md.

Captain John Rogers, at Spotsylvania, C. H., Va.

Jos. Singleton, at Petersburg, Va.

Noah Smith, at Brandy Station, Va.

John M. Walker, at Gettysburg, Pa.

John S. Withrow, at Strasburg, Va.

The following died of disease :

Corporal J. B. Findley, W. G. Austin, J. W. Appleton, A. B. Brindley, J. G. Beeson, J. M. Burnett, W. C. Brandon, G. Cunningham, J. C. Clayton, Peter Carroll, C. E. Drake, D. H. Duff, L. A. Dobbs, Thomas Dutton, J. K. P. Estes, F. M. Edwards, A. A. Fulcher, J. C. Fletcher, J. B. Frazier, J. P. Hunter, R. S. Hulgin, D. W. Kennedy, B. F. Lewis, A. W Langford, S. M. McSpadden, T. K. B. McSpadden, M. Murphy, G. McPherson, I. R. Pendergrass, J. M. Sutherland, J. L. Ward.

From the above list will be seen the great mortality experienced by this patriotic company

Mr. Brandon, in his souvenir book, states that the company participated in the battles of Seven Pines, Cold Harbor, Gaines' Mills, Frazier's Farm, Malvern Hill, Boonsboro, Sharpsburg, Chancellorsville, Winchester, Wilderness, Fredericksburg, Gettysburg, Hagerstown, Petersburg, Strasburg, Mine Run, Snicker's Gap, Martinsburg, Warrenton C. H., Spotsylvania C. H., and Appomattox C. H., besides many severe skirmishes that could not be called battles. In these battles all the other companies of the Regiment also participated.

"Macon Confederates," Company F, Macon County.

Captain Robert F. Ligon. Elected to the Senate of Alabama and resigned April, 1862. Afterward elected Lieutenant-Governor of Alabama, and member of the United States Congress. Died in Montgomery, Ala., November, 1902, universally loved and lamented.

Captain Robert H. Keeling. Killed at Seven Pines. See sketch of him elsewhere.

Captain John W. McNeely. Wounded at Chancellorsville. Retired and placed on conscript duty in 1S64. President of Soule University, Texas. Died about 1889.

Captain Robert E. Park. Wounded slightly at the Wilderness 5th of May, severely wounded at Gettysburg and Winchester, and left in the hands of the enemy. Three times elected treasurer of Georgia. Living at present in Atlanta, Ga.

First Lieutenants: R. H. Keeling, J. W McNeely, R.E. Park.

Second Lieutenants: W. D. Zuber, not re-elected: George Jones, not re-elected; J. B. Fletcher, killed at Sharpsburg; J. W Wright, resigned in 1863 and left the country; G. W. Wright, wounded at Gettysburg and retired; died as result of wounds about 1868.

Company F.

The following were killed: Captain R. H. Keeling, First Lieut. E. P. Hendree, who was discharged and afterward promoted to First Lieut, in 61st Alabama, and killed 5th of May, 1864, at the Wilderness.

J. H. Attaway, mortally wounded and died, Winchester, Va.

J. T. Black, mortally wounded at Chancellorsville.

W. T. Cooper, killed near Petersburg.

M. A. Flournoy, mortally wounded at Seven Pines and died.

J. U. Ingram, killed at Seven Pines.

J. M. Lester, killed at Petersburg.

William Mimms, killed at Cedar Creek, October 19, 1864.
Corporal J. B. Nuckolls, killed at Sharpsburg, September 17, 1862.
John Preskitt, killed at Gettysburg.
Ensign R. H. Stafford, killed at Cedar Creek, October 19, 1864.
W B. (Tobe) Ward, killed near Petersburg.
P W Chappell, killed at Petersburg.
Lucius Williams, killed at Winchester.
Isaac Eason, killed 19th May near Spotsylvania C. H.
J. T Eberhart, killed at Snicker's Gap, July 18, 1864.
William Howard, killed at Petersburg.

The following died of wounds or disease: S. M. Blackburn, C. H. Cobb, B. Fitzpatrick, G. P Grimmett, M. G. Holloway, H. H. McPhaul, W A. Noble, P. Philpot, W P Bowdon, W F. Chesson, J. M. Germany, A. A. Gillespie, R. L. Hairston, W J. Moody, R. J. Nobles, died in prison, S. L. Roberts, S. G. Starke, R. T. Simmons, M. W Wright R. P. Wynn, E. H. Strobell, A. J. Veasey, C. F Wagner.

The following have died since the war: R. F Ligon, Geo. Jones, J H. Echols, who was Colonel of the 63rd Ala; A. S. Grigg, who was discharged from service; J. W McNeely, J. R. Flewellen, was discharged in 1862; J. A. Cunningham, obtained substitute in 1862; J. R. Adams, H. J. Attaway, discharged 1861; A. J. Blount, discharged 1863; S. B. Brewer, sutler, died in Texas; W H. Bilbro discharged; David Clopton, promoted Quarter Master, elected to Confederate Congress, died while Justice of the Supreme Court of Alabama; W. F. Chesson, Serg. W. M. Carr, wounded and retired; J. W. Fannin, promoted Captain of 61st Alabama; Corp. R. R. Grimmett, obtained substitute; T. S. Crawford, M. Moore, F. A. Manning, W. P. Zachry, H. R. Thorpe, promoted Surgeon; T. M. Kimbrough, W. F. Moore, in Texas; E. A. Ligon, promoted Surgeon; Corporal A. Wilkerson, J. Johnson, in 1861, W R. Tompkins, J. R. Scroggins, N. R. Simmons, died December 9, 1904. S. H. Slaton, B. F. Smith, Sergeant A. P. Reid, in Texas. D. Oswalt, N. Richardson, died in 1904, 97 years of age; Dr. G. W McElhany, T. N. Kesterson, }. Patterson.

Rev. E. J. Rogers, right leg shot off at Gettysburg.
B. F Ingram, in Texas, 1903.
Corporal Henderson, died in 1868, editor *Tuskegee News*.
J. H. Upshavv.
B. F. Ward, arm shot off at Chancellorsville.
A. G. Howard, promoted Ordnance Sergeant, died in Atlanta, Ga. J. S. Porter, 1905.

As far as the writer can ascertain only the following are now surviving:

Captain R. E. Park, Atlanta, Ga.

T. H. Clower, who commanded the company the last eight months of the war, Opelika, Ala.

H. G. Lamar, Iredell, Texas.

Dr. J. F. Park, LaGrange, Ga.

R. F. Segrest, Hico, Texas.

R. W. Drake, Laneville, Ala., late sheriff of Hale county.

C. C. Davis, Tuskegee, Ala. J. H. Eason, Tallassee, Ala. G. P. Ware, Auburn, Ala. G. W. Ward, Willhite, La.

Rev. W. A. Moore, Neches, Texas.

Fletch. S. Zachry. Tyler, Texas.

W. D. Zuber, Pine Level, Ala.

J. R. Walker, Dallas, Ga.

C. B. Florence, Golden City. Ark., Colonel UCV

Company G, "Paint Rock River Sharpshooters" Jackson County.

Captain A. S. Bibb, resigned early.

Captain J J. Dillard, killed on Sand Mountain, Ala., in 1S63. Captain P D. Ross, who remained Captain until the close of the war, surrendering with Lee. Captain Daniel Butler, died.

First Lieutenants: John J. Dillard, Rufus H. Jones, P D. Ross, John S. Dudley, killed.

Second Lieutenants: R. H. Jones, Abner Hammond, killed at Seven Pines; Daniel Butler, J. M. Hardcastle, died after the war of wounds received at Seven Pines; J. M. Fletcher.

Captain P D. Ross and Lieutenant J. M. Fletcher of Company G, were both wounded, as I was, at the battle of Gettysburg, and with Captain Hewlett of Company H, and Lieutenant George W Wright, of my company — F, were occupants of the same tent near an old barn used as a field hospital, and during the night of the 3rd of July, 1863, I occupied a blanket near Lieutenant Fletcher, who had been shot through the body, and was suffering greatly, moaning and groaning during the night so that I was constantly inquiring whether I could do anything for his relief, and being told each time that nothing could be done. During the latter part of the night I slept, and upon waking the next day I found him lying by my side, cold in death. He was a quiet, modest, brave young officer.

This company had among its members a well known corporal

named Henry Fowler. While we were in winter quarters, on one occasion he was detailed with two men from the Twelfth Alabama, as Brigade Headquarter Guard for General Rodes. General Rodes had a twenty-five pound turkey given him and had invited some of the brigadiers and colonels in his command to a dinner. It was a current story that this superb gobbler, done to a crisp, with dressing and gravy, but no doubt without cranberries and celery, was on the table in a tent adjoining the General's sleeping quarters, and, while steaming hot, the cook invited the company to the table. In some mysterious way, before they could walk the ten or fifteen feet necessary to reach the table, the magnificent bird was wafted out of sight and never more seen, at least by General Rodes, or any of his company. The General is reported to have become very angry with Corporal Fowler and his two brother guards, and expressed himself in very positive language, and during this talk he spoke of Fowler as belonging to the "damned thieving Twelfth Alabama." This not very complimentary appellation abided with the Twelfth Alabama, from the time of this incident to the close of the war.

The Germans, French, Irish and Spaniards, and old sailors from Mobile, and the mountain boys from North Alabama, who composed a large portion of the Twelfth Alabama, were noted as foragers, and the vast majority of them suffered very little from hunger, despite frequently limited rations issued to the regiment by the commissary. Many a time I have been aroused by Dick Noble, Wesley Moore, Wat. Zachry, Jim Lester and others of my company, when we were in bivouac, before the bugle sounded for a day's march, and told that I must get up and eat some fried chicken, or assist them in eating some biscuits and honey, which I was told had been presented (?) to them by some patriotic Virginian living near by.

Company G was made up at Woodville and Paint Rock in the southwest corner of Jackson county, with several members from East Madison and North Marshall counties. They left Woodville for Richmond, Va., the 26th of June, 1861.

When the Company was re-organized at Yorktown, Captain Bibb and Lieutenants Jones and Dillard were not re-elected.

I can find no record of what became of Captain Bibb.

Lieutenant Dillard became a recruiting officer, and was killed by Union men or Tories in the winter of 1864.

Lieutenant Jones joined the Confederate forces of North Alabama and served through the war.

At the re-organization Daniel Butler was elected Captain, P. D. Ross, First Lieutenant, J. M. Hardcastle, Second Lieutenant, and Abner Hammond Jr., Second Lieutenant.

In a few weeks Captain Butler sickened and died, and on the 31st of May at Seven Pines Lieutenant Hammond was killed.

Early in June Lieutenant Ross was made Captain and John S. Dudley and J. M. Fletcher were elected lieutenants.

Lieutenant Dudley was killed at Chancellorsville on Saturday evening, the first day of the battle, and Lieutenant Fletcher was killed, as heretofore described, at Gettysburg.

The first man in Company G that was killed was Dr. Solomon G. Stevens. He had been transferred to the 9th Alabama as regimental surgeon, and was killed by a shell thrown in the camp near Yorktown. The next one to fall was Lieutenant Hammond at Seven Pines, and Sergt. Richard Bevil, privates George Kirkland, Rufus Crawley, N. T. Clifton, Jefferson Atchley, Michael Hoke and Thomas Smith. Private William Middleton and Mike Swister were killed near Culpepper C. H. Thomas Rogers and Stuart were killed at South Mountain. James Posey, W. H. Burks, Abner Riggins, Edward Bevil and A. J. Grizzle were killed at Sharpsburg. W. J. Rogers, Ben Taylor and Brooks Taylor were killed at Gettysburg. Private Samuel Kennemer and Silas Wright were subsequently killed.

Captain P. D. Ross became a teacher at Alexandria, Ala., after the war and also became clerk of the Circuit Court and was a deservedly popular and efficient officer, dying at Jacksonville, Ala., a few years ago.

Company H, Morgan County.

Captain B. B. Gayle. Elected lieutenant-colonel at Yorktown. Promoted colonel after the death of Colonel Jones. Killed at Boonsboro.

Captain J. H. Darwin. Promoted to captain at Yorktown. Killed at Seven Pines.

Captain M. B. Robinson, Jr. Promoted to captain after Seven Pines. Resigned after the battle of Sharpsburg.

Captain A. E. Hewlett. Elected from private to second lieutenant after retreat from Yorktown. Promoted to first lieutenant after Seven Pines, and to captain after Sharpsburg. Lives at Cullman, Ala. Editor of a paper and Register of the Court of Chancery. A very popular and excellent citizen.

First Lieutenants: J. H. Darwin; E. Ryan, promoted at Yorktown, killed at Seven Pines; A. E. Hewlett.

Second Lieutenant J. D. Graham. Elected from ranks second lieutenant after Seven Pines, resigned after Sharpsburg, died near Huntsville.

Second Lieutenant J. D. Spain. Wounded and disabled at Sharpsburg.

Second Lieutenant J. S. Brittain. Resigned. Died after the war near Decatur, Ala.

Second Lieutenant David Sams. Killed November 19, 1864, in the Valley of Virginia.

The following members of this company were killed in battle:
E. Brown, Seven Pines.
Dock Bishop, at Gettysburg.
Tom Dunn, at Seven Pines.
William Harris, at Seven Pines.
J. Hamilton, at Boonsboro.
F. M. Hamilton, at Spotsylvania.
Lud Hall, at Boonsboro.
Wm. Halbrooks, at Gaines Mill.
Sam Heflin, at Seven Pines.
Wyatt Martin, at Snicker's Gap.
Dick Priddy, at Seven Pines.
Carrol Ryan, at Gettysburg.
Jas. Ryan, died of wounds in Richmond hospital.
Nath. Smith, at Seven Pines.
Jourdan Waid, at Seven Pines.

The following died since the war:

J. L. Box, assassinated; J. H. Burt, Wm. Campbell, died in hospital at Richmond; Sim Garrett, J. R. Herring, died in hospital; Jesse Herring, Andrew Jenkins, Jack Little, J. Lemons, S. Lassiter, John McAnear, Dow Prater, Mac. Rominez, John Rominez, R. Ward, Frank Woods.

Private J. F Winds obtained a substitute. Joined General Roddy's cavalry. Was elected lieutenant colonel. Since died.

Company I, "Southern Foresters," Mobile County.

Captain Wm. T Walthall, John J. Nicholson, E. H. Jones.

First Lieutenans John J. Nicholson, L. Walthall, afterwards Quarter Master for a short time.

Second Lieutenants E. H. Jones, J. O. Patton.

This Company was organized in June, 1861, left Mobile for the front July 4th, 1861.

First Lieutenant Nicholson became captain in May, 1862, on the resignation of Capt. Walthall. The latter was an accomplished teacher and scholar, and for a long time connected as editor with the *Mobile Register*. He assisted President Jefferson Davis in the preparation of his wonderful book, *The Rise and Fall of the Confederate States*.

This company was composed largely of young men who were employed around the wharves of Mobile and connected with the steamships and boating. They had a peculiar uniform of dark gray with blue trimmings.

Bruce R. Davis, of this company, was for some time the sergeant major of the regiment and a very bright man, who wrote a very beautiful hand.

Among the privates of the company was Edward W. Pettus, who bore the same name as the present United States Senator from Alabama, General E. W. Pettus. I have no record of what became of him.

Lieutenant J. O. Patton was a native of Portland, Me., and a very gallant soldier and officer. He had the Down Easter brogue, and, later on, I will mention an incident in his career at the battle of Chickahominy.

Porter L. Myers went out as the Third Corporal of Company I, and was killed by my side, while we were fighting Hatch's Pennsylvania Bucktails on South Mountain. A very extended mention of this incident is given under the head of the "Battle of Boonesboro."

Company K, "Tom Watts' Rebels," Macon County.

This company was formed at Auburn, Ala., in May and June, 1861. The first captain was Prof. William H. C. Price, a graduate of the University of Alabama, an educator and editor of prominence, residing at Auburn. He was the youngest brother of Rev. G. W. F. Price, D. D., of Nashville, Tenn., and son-in-law of the renowned scholar, Prof. John Darby. LL. D.

The first lieutenant was William S. Goodwyn, a prominent planter of La Place, who subsequently became colonel of the 45th Alabama.

William A. Scott, a young lawyer of Auburn, and now judge of Clay county court, at Fort Gaines, Ga., was second lieutenant.

William Himes, a very bright and promising young man of eighteen years, was junior second lieutenant.

By August 15th the roll of this company, including officers and men, contained one hundred names.

About the 20th of July the company left Auburn for Richmond, and camped near the other companies of the regiment with which it was soon united, near the reservoir.

Company K joined the other nine companies of the 12th Alabama at Camp Walker, near Centreville, Va., early in August.

Dr. D. S. Patterson, a prominent citizen and druggist of Montgomery, Ala., carried a squad of this company from Pike county, reaching Virginia about the 15th of August.

This company was named "Tom Watts' Rebels" after Attorney General T. H. Watts of President Davis' Cabinet, and later one of the war governors of Alabama, who assisted in procuring its organization and equipment. The following is a list of the officers:

Captains: William H. C. Price, resigned after one year's service; D. H. Garrison, E. H. Rowell.

First Lieutenants: W. S. Goodwyn, B. F. O'Neal, now an honored citizen of South Sulphur, Tex.; J. Thomas Scott, promoted from sergeant and resigned, now dead; D. H. Garrison, E. H. Rowell, now living at Funston, Tex., a physician.

Second Lieutenants Wm. A. Scott, resigned; Wm. Himes, resigned, recently Railroad Commissioner of Florida, and a popular citizen of that State, lives at Bushnell, Florida.

Twelfth Alabamians who Surrendered at Appomattox, April 9th, 1865.

Below I copy from Volume XV, pages 244-46 of the *Southern Historical Society Papers* a list of the paroles issued to the members of the Twelfth Alabama. It is a pitifully small list and painfully shows how dreadfully this noble band of heroic soldiers had diminished from the eleven hundred and ninety-six which formed the regiment on the 12th of June, 1861. These names deserve to be emblazoned forever on the rolls of fame, and to go down in history with the brave Spartans who fought at Thermopylae.

Of those who survive now from this list I can only locate a few. Among those are:

Sergeant George W. Thomas of Company B, who lives near Alexander city, in Coosa county, Alabama.

Sergeant James H. Eason of Company F, who lives at Tallassee, Alabama.

Private William A. Moore of Company F, who lives in Neches, Texas.

Dr. Daniel S. Patterson of Company K, who lives at Montgomery, Ala. The post offices of the others are not known to me, and I deeply regret that I cannot put them in this list.

Those who surrendered, as given in this book of "Paroles", are as follows:

Twelfth Alabama Regiment

Company A.

Privates: John Arnold, T S. Hazzard, detailed shoemaker, John Ford, Reuben Popewell.

Company B.

Sergeants: George W Thomas, Richard H. Corley, detailed division Provost Guard.

Corporal John H. Phillips.

Privates: Robert L. Goodgame, David C. Hogan, James W. Hollinshaw, William B. Hardagree, Thomas Jacobs, Oliver P. Looney, John McKay, teamster, John O. McPherson, Robert H. J. Mallory, Benjamin F. Pinson.

Company C.

Sergeant Calvin Hoyt.

Privates: Reuben C. Edwards, Anderson McGraw, John G. Williams, William T. Walker, Robert Esterheld, division commissary department.

Company D.

Corporal Wade H. Cardwell.

Privates: James M. Buzby. Henry R. Cook, James P. McClenny, Jesse Pritchett, Robert Turner.

Company E.

Sergeant Robert B. Kirk.

Corporal Amos A. Cox.

Privates: John Tachett, detailed teamster, Jasper Rogers.

Company F

Sergeants: James H. Eason, Azariah G. Howard, Orderly Ser- geant 1 2th Alabama.

Privates: Thomas W Collier, Micajah J. Moore, William A. Moore, Asbury F Manning, James A. Parker, detailed teamster.

Company G.

Privates: Jasper W. Sawyer, detailed teamster, Chas. R. Smith, Green Swearingin, detailed teamster.

Company H.

Corporal Jesse Herring.
Privates: Andrew P. Calhoun, division Provost Guard, Lawson C. Meeks, Simon Mayor, Levi N. Oden, William Odom, Dock R. Priddy. John W. Rantz, detailed harness maker.

Company I.

Sergeant: Wesley Thomas, William Corbett. Musician Henry C. Sweetzer.

Company K.

Privates: Chester W Abercrombie, Ernest Buhler, detailed shoemaker, Thomas Craddock, Robert Marion, Jas. E. Morrison, Albert W Seay, Daniel S. Patterson.

The Yorktown Election and Reorganization.

April 28th, 1862, orders were received from the War Department, at Richmond, permitting and directing the re-organization of all the twelve-months companies which had enlisted for the war. This order created a great deal of excitement and intense interest among the soldiers, particularly the Twelfth Alabama, nearly every company in which had enlisted for only twelve months.

Colonel Robert T. Jones, of Marion, Ala., a native of Richmond, Va., a graduate of West Point, and a very accomplished soldier, who had been a captain in the United States army, was a candidate for re-election, and opposed by Captain A. Stikes of Company C, from Mobile.

Captain R. H. Keeling, of Company F, was a candidate for lieutenant colonel, and opposed by Captain L. D. Patterson of Company E. Captain Keeling was a graduate of the Virginia Military Institute and had as his schoolmates General R. E. Rodes, General R. E. Colston and other distinguished officers.

Captain B. B. Gayle, of Company H, who had military training at Portsmouth, Va., and had been teaching in Morgan county. Ala., was a candidate for major.

The result of the election was the choice of R. T Jones for colonel, L. D. Patterson for lieutenant colonel, and B B. Gayle for major.

The defeat of Captain Keeling for lieutenant colonel by Captain Patterson, who was an excellent soldier, having been promoted from private in his company to captain, and who was a teacher of good repute in North Alabama, greatly surprised the officers and many of the men in the regiment, as there was no doubt of the superior qualifications of Captain Keeling for the position. Colonel Jones was so disturbed and indignant that he refused to recommend Captain Patterson for the position of lieutenant colonel, and the consequence was that Captain Patterson declined to contest for the place and resigned from his company and regiment. This caused another election and B. B. Carle was elected lieutenant-colonel, and Adjutant S. B. Pickens was elected major.

The day before the election, Captain Keeling came to my tent, where I was sitting in conversation with Orderly Sergeant John W McNeely, my mess-mate, and astonished me by asking me why I did not run for second lieutenant. I replied that I was a Georgian, in an Alabama regiment, and had not entertained the thought of such an aspiration. He replied: "You can be easily elected, for I have been talking among the men about it." He then informed me that the understanding was that Captain R. F. Ligon, who had been elected to the Alabama Senate, would decline a re-election to the captaincy, and that he himself would be elected captain without opposition; that Sergeant McNeely would be elected first lieutenant, and that it was believed that neither Lieutenant Zuber nor Lieutenant Jones would be candidates for re-election, and that the company were undecided as to who should be elected second and third lieutenants.

Encouraged by this conversation, and advice, I acted upon Lieutenant Keeling's suggestion and visited each one of the occupants of the nine tents used by members of Company F.

The first tent, or number one, fortunately, had its members sitting down ready for dinner, and I recall that there were present Sergeant M. A. Flournoy, of Opelika, Corporal E. P. Hendree, of Tuskegee, later promoted to first lieutenant in the Sixty-first Alabama regiment, and killed at the Wilderness on the 5th of May Private James W. Fannin, of Tuskegee, afterwards captain in the Sixty-first Alabama. Private A. Fuller Henderson, son of the distinguished Baptist minister, Rev. Samuel Henderson, D. D., of Tuskegee, and who afterwards became editor and proprietor of the *Tuskegee News*, and who killed himself, whether intentionally or accidentally, is unknown, in 1867. Private Robert F. Hall, of Auburn, afterwards first sergeant, and who was wounded in the foot at Chancellorsville and retired from service, becoming foreman of the *Montgomery Advertiser*, being an accomplished printer. Private Robert W Drake, now of Laneville, Ala., and perhaps two or three others.

In response to my statement that I would be a candidate for

second lieutenant at the election the following day, the boys instantly spoke up and told me that they would vote for me.

I then visited the second tent in which were equally as good friends, and some of them former college mates at Auburn, as in the first tent, among them being Private Thomas H. Clower, of Auburn, afterwards orderly sergeant of Company F, and recommended during the latter days of the war for a commission as second lieutenant, and who has recently been the popular mayor of Opelika, and is one of her most esteemed and highly respected citizens, a thorough gentleman and a brave and intrepid soldier. Private S. B. Brewer, of Tuskegee, afterwards regimental sutler. Private J. B. Fletcher, afterwards elected third lieutenant, and killed at Sharpsburg, Md. Private R. H. Stafford, afterwards the color sergeant of the regiment, and killed at Cedar Creek, Va., October 19, 1864. Corporal A. G. Howard, afterwards desperately wounded and promoted to ordnance sergeant of the regiment, and who died in Atlanta, Ga., where he had become a prominent and wealthy merchant, a few years ago. He had risen to the position of Grand Chief Templar of the Grand Commandery of Knight Templars of Georgia, and one of Georgia's most excellent citizens.

Upon making known my purpose to these young friends, they responded as did tent number one, and promised their cordial support.

I then visited the other seven tents in the line and spoke, among others, to James M. Lester, who was killed near Appomattox C. H., just before the surrender. Private W F Moore, who died recently in Texas; Private William Mimms, who was killed at Cedar Creek, Va., October 19th, 1864; Walter O. Nicholson, who was later discharged, under age; Dick Nobles who died at Elmira, N. Y., a prisoner, in 1865; Dan Oswalt who died since the war; John Preeskitt, who was killed at Gettysburg July 1st, 1863; Nat Richardson, who was discharged soon after for being over age, and died in 1904; A. P. Reid, afterwards second sergeant of the company and died in Texas three or four years ago; Ben F. Smith, the best fiddler I believe in the Army of Northern Virginia, an old bachelor, who died a few years since; Nathan R. Simmons of Opelika, who became a sergeant and died in Opelika, holding the position of superintendent of public works, in December, 1904; Dr. H. R. Thorpe, of Auburn, who later was promoted to assistant-surgeon of a North Carolina regiment; J. W. Wright, who was elected third lieutenant next day, but left the company and the Confederacy very soon after; George W. Wright, who was afterwards elected second lieutenant and retired on account of wound received in the head at Gettysburg, and died afterwards at Loachapoka, Ala.; George Pierce Ware, of Auburn, Ala., the brave, Christian soldier who was often wounded but is now living, a highly respected citizen, six miles from Auburn, Ala.; W. B. (Tobe) Ward, who was killed near Appomattox, Va.; Corporal Archy Wilkerson, who was badly wounded in the mouth, and died in Arkansas since the war, and the two gallant brothers, Walter P. and Fletcher Zachry. The latter is now living, a respected citizen of Tyler, Texas. Moses W Wright, of Tuskegee, who died later during the war, and the two brave brothers, John U. and Ben. F. Ingram.

John was killed at Seven Pines May 31, 1862, just one month later, and Ben died at Garrison, Tex., in 1903.

Among all of these comrades I met a cordial reception, except at the hands of Corp. Wilkerson, who, speaking for his tent number 9, replied: "We have no objection to you, but if Lieutenant Zuber, who comes from our settlement, is a candidate, our mess will have to vote for him." I replied that the men in the other eight tents were unanimous for me and that I did not feel any concern if the lieutenant did decide to become a candidate.

The next day's result of the election in Company F was:

Robert H. Keeling, captain; John W. McNeely, first lieutenant; Robert E. Park, second lieutenant — all unanimously; John W. Wright elected third lieutenant over Sergeant M. A. Flournoy, A. S. Grigg and R. Flewellen.

The election of field officers, and the prompt refusal of Colonel Jones to endorse Captain Patterson as lieutenant colonel caused intense excitement, but it soon wore away.

The second day after my election I was detailed to act as officer of the guard, and reported in my private's uniform, with a borrowed sword, to Colonel Jones. The colonel glanced up and looked at me from head to foot, and from foot to head, and quaintly said, "I am glad, Lieutenant, that you were elected a commissioned officer, but I advise you to get a new uniform as soon as possible." He then quietly gave me instructions as to my new duties. It is a source of regret that I could not preserve a photograph or ambrotype of myself as I appeared when I reported to Colonel Jones. I was something over seventeen years of age. I had grown considerably and my round-a-bout gray coat had become too short and did not meet my pants, nor could it be but- toned in front. The end of the sleeves was fully six inches from my hand. The pants had been scorched in the rear, on the calf of the leg, and were a mass of dark strings. The bottom of the trousers was fully four inches above my worn out, soleless shoes. My soft wool hat was battered and torn until it didn't deserve to be dignified by the name of hat. It was scarcely a head covering. A few days after this election we began our retreat between the York and James Rivers to Chickahominy swamp, via Williamsburg, and in passing the 14th North Carolina I overheard this remark loudly spoken by one "Tar Heel" to another: "Look there, boys, see that uniform? There goes your new election." I was trudging along by the side of my company in the same uniform in which I had saluted Col. Jones, and with the borrowed sword buckled around me. The dilapidated condition of the whole regiment was a constant source of humorous remarks, not only by those who composed but by all who saw it. But they were not alone in this particular. The army at Yorktown was one clothed in rags.

The Battle of Williamsburg.

Yorktown was evacuated by Johnston May 4, 1862, at night. He marched steadily, but was delayed by mud, rain, slush and boggy roads caused by wagon and artillery trains.

Rodes' Brigade, during the afternoon of the next day, heard the firing of cannon and hastened forward in the direction of the fighting. As we passed through the Old Capital of Virginia, the doors, windows, balconies and sidewalks were crowded with beautiful women and children who were wild with excitement, waving handkerchiefs and flags and handing us sandwiches, fresh water, etc., and speaking encouraging words. The men became enthusiastic, the very air rang with our shouts, and we pressed forward eager for the conflict. We hurried to the field, and were formed in line in the rear of General Early's command. Artillery and musketry and the shouts and shrieks of men; some in the tongues of triumph and others in those of pain, greeted us as we rushed along. Minie balls flew over the heads of our brave comrades in front, but none of our men were seriously wounded and we were not actively engaged.

Darkness fell and put an end to the fray, It was an unhappy night, we were wet and faint with hunger and fatigue. It was cold and we kept stamping our feet, marking time, and crowding together in groups to keep warm, as we halted and then moved on.

It was a memorable May day, this 5th of the month, and was our first actual experience in war. We marched before day through Williamsburg, and the men literally waded almost knee deep in mud, as the road was rendered almost impassable from the constant rains and stirred by the artillery and baggage trains. I can never forget that some of my men, in pulling their feet along, left their shoes in the mud, and the rough words that came from Miller McCraw still ringing my ears, as I took his gun and knapsack and carried them for him. He was only 15 years old, and ought to have been at home at school.

The next day we had a new experience, that of eating parched corn, for our rations did not come up until late. Slowly we continued the retreat, or advance, as you may prefer to call it, and on the 13th of May we came to the Chickahominy river. Here we had a few drills, and the first day, I recall, that all of us, of the newly elected officers, were very ignorant of our duties, and when we were forming into divisions composed of two companies, as both Captain Keeling and Lieutenant McNeely were absent, I was thrown in command of Company F, and the captain of the company next to mine should have been in command of the division, but, with an imploring look, he placed himself along the line and called to me to take command of the division, that he didn't know what to do. Though I had but little more acquaintance with tactics than he, I had a little more assurance, and I assumed command of the division and held it until the close of a prolonged drill.

Next day I was sent with a squad of men to report to Major Early, a tall, dark-skinned, civil engineer, said to be a brother of General J. A. Early, and to assist in the construction of a pontoon bridge across the Chickahominy.

Seven Pines.

May 30, 1862, was warm and sultry. The Twelfth Alabama was kept under arms, and moved about frequently, as if expecting a battle. After sunset we went into bivouac and were ordered to prepare rations for the next day. The men were busy until very late that night, and then, tired out, they sought rest. Very soon a terrible thunderstorm arose. It sounded as if heaven and earth were in conflict, while the rain fell in sheets and torrents. The men were poorly sheltered, many with little fly tents, others with only a single blanket on a pole, a poor substitute for a tent. This dreadful night, with its terrific storm raging, its sheets of lightning and torrents of rain, its sharp and deafening thunder, was a forerunner of the bloody strife to wage the next two days. The roads were deep with mud and water, and the woods and fields held water as high as our ankles, and often went to our knees, and even to our waists.

May 31 and June 1, 1862, found General Joe Johnston and General McClellan fronting each other and fighting the great two-days battle of Seven Pines, called by some "Fair Oaks." This was one of the most desperate, hotly contested and bloody fields of the war. In the morning we noticed many federal balloons flying in the air taking observations. McClellan had 100,000 splendidly equipped soldiers, while Johnston had only 63,000. Our losses were 6,134 killed and wounded, and the federals lost 5,031, making a total of 11,165 brave men. The storm passed away on the morning of the 31st, leaving the air cool and bracing. It was a lovely May morning and the sun rose bright and clear. Though they were wet, and had enjoyed little sleep, the men were full of life and courage, and the woods resounded with their cheerful voices and brisk movements. Breakfast was soon enjoyed and the order "fall in" was given. The Twelfth Alabama numbered 408 men and officers present for duty, and was led by Colonel R. T. Jones, Lieutenant Colonel B. B. Gayle, Major S. B. Pickens, while Captain R. H. Keeling commanded Company F, and I, as second lieutenant, accompanied our command, while Lieutenant McNeely was acting commissary of the regiment. Lieutenant Wright was also absent.

The Fifth Alabama under command of Colonel C. C. Pegues, Lieutenant Colonel J. M. Hall, and Major E. L. Hobson; the Sixth Alabama under Colonel John B. Gordon, Lieutenant Colonel B. H. Baker, and Major Nesmith; the Twelfth Mississippi under Colonel N. H. Harris, afterwards promoted to brigadier general. These regiments composed, with the Twelfth Alabama, Rodes' Brigade.

Early in the morning we were drawn up in front of the enemy's works under cover of a dense forest, within one-fourth of a mile of the enemy's batteries and redoubts. These redoubts bristled with artillery, and were supported by numerous infantry and flanked by breastworks. We moved forward through the mud, water and limbs of trees, cut down to form obstructions to our approach, and, as we moved, the enemy opened on us with their artillery, and a dreadful storm of shot, shell, grape and cannister tore through the trees, plowing up the ground on every side and cutting off limbs and small trees above and around us. We moved on to the assault, and under the terrible fire of musketry and artillery which we could not return, because of the abatis in our front, and the difficulty of getting over them, but the brave and devoted men kept moving forward, until at last an open field was reached near the enemy's works. The men were placed in a hurried line of battle, and continued to rush upon the enemy, who seemed to renew their firing with redoubled fury. Our men fell rapidly, some dying, many dead, and others dangerously wounded.

I heard the clarion voice of Colonel Gordon calling to his men on our right, above the roar of battle. His major, Nesmith, was killed. Capt. Bell and 44 of his men were killed or wounded in one company.

The 12th's old superb commander, Col. R T. Jones, was instantly killed. But we silenced the battery in front of us, rushed through the moat of water, climbed over the breastwork, ran through the tents, vacated by Gen. Casey's troops, and moved on beyond the camp, halting in front of a collection of abatis, which was formed by cutting down a dense grove of old field pines and trimming and sharpening the limbs so as to impede our progress. While lying down here we could see the enemy a short distance in front, despite the smoke of battle, and it was at this point that Capt. Keeling was instantly killed. Private Nicholson called out to me: "Lieut. Park, Capt. Keeling is killed, you must take command of the company." I rose, walked down the line of the company and urged the men to avenge the death of our captain.

Kneeling by the side of Serg. Flournoy, of Opelika, and private J. W. Fannin, of Tuskegee, I heard Flournoy call to Fannin: "Shoot that officer in front of you." In response, Fannin gazed intently before him, but soon remarked that he could not see him. Flournoy's reply was, "The mischief you can't, I do," and with that he raised his gun, and deliberately pointing, fired; at the same time he received a bullet through the top of his head, laying his brains bare.

We continued firing for some minutes, until it became almost too dark to distinguish the enemy in front, and were then ordered to retire behind the redoubts now in our rear. I let the entire company fall back before I started, and, taking the hand of Sergt. Flournoy in mine, I said, "Mack, dear fellow, I am sorry to lose you, but you see I am alone and must go." The poor fellow paralyzed by his wound, was unable to speak, but pressed my hand cordially and closed his eyes in assent, while the big tears rolled down his noble face. Then, leaving him, I hurriedly ran to overtake my comrades, and miraculously escaped the thousands of minie balls that were being hurled above and around me.

It was appalling to see how few men formed in line with us after dark, how reduced we were in numbers. The strong, orderly line of the morning was now scarcely more than a line of skirmishers, and from 408 had been reduced to 203 present for duty, making a loss of 205 men from our single command. The ground seemed literally covered with the dead and wounded.

This was our first experience in real battle. The men were worn out, and were glad to stretch themselves upon the wet ground and slept soundly, though the air was filled with the agonizing cries and groans of the wounded and dying men and animals by whom they were surrounded. It is impossible for me to describe or properly eulogize the splendid conduct of the officers and men in this notable engagement. They showed coolness, deliberation, daring, in making their way through the pointed abatis while suffering from the galling fire at short range. I can never forget the calm resolve with which the men reformed their line after we had reached the open field, within a hundred feet of the enemy's breastworks. They did not wince nor dodge under the terrible and destructive fire, but, with the utmost coolness and precision, returned it, undisturbed by their trying situation. The gallant charge they made into the very jaws of death while crossing the works and through the forsaken camp, their stubborn courage as they retired, evinced a lofty heroism worthy of patriots of any age and any country. The names of these martyr patriots may never be recorded in history or known to fame, but it seems to me that such men not only illustrated their own states and section, but they ennobled humanity The world was poorer by their loss.

Rev. Dr. J. L. Burrows, the distinguished Baptist minister, and many noble citizens of Richmond, spent the night walking among the wounded, relieving their necessities. The ambulance corps did not sleep, but were busy carrying the wounded into Richmond.

Early next morning I saw an ambulance pass by, and was attracted by the sight of a weeping negro man walking behind it, and recognized Mark, the cook and slave of Sergeant Flournoy. He had learned of his master's wound and had been with him all night, and was then following the ambulance, as it was being driven into the city. As he passed Company F, and saw us preparing breakfast, he burst into tears and it was a tender and pathetic sight to witness his great grief over the condition of his beloved master. Sergeant Flournoy lived for a week in Chimborazo Hospital, conscious to the last, able to recognize any one, but wholly unable to speak, and then calmly gave up his generous and patriotic spirit. My gallant cousin, Colonel G. A. Bull, of the Thirty-Fifth Georgia, was killed bravely cheering on his men.

My own beloved Captain Keeling gave up, as I have stated, his life during the battle. His clear, ringing voice I can hear now, calling to and inspiring the men on that memorable battlefield. In speaking of Captain Keeling I am but obeying an irresistible impulse of my heart. He was my friend, ever generous and kind to me. We marched and fought side by side, and on that woeful and never-to-be-forgotten day, the 31st of May. 1862, amid the tempest of fire and hail of iron, he fell within a few feet of me, and his noble spirit winged its eternal flight to the land of the hereafter. Captain Keeling was born in Richmond, Va. His father, the Rev. Henry Keeling, D. D., was a noted Baptist minister, and for years editor of a church paper. He was a poet of no mean reputation. Captain Keeling's education was received mainly at the Virginia Military Institute.

Soon after his graduation, at the age of 19, the Mexican war having broken out, he was chosen 1st lieutenant of a company of Virginia Infantry, and hastened to the scene of action. He commanded his company and acted as adjutant for twenty-two months in the regiment in which General Early was major. When the Mexican war was over he adopted teaching as a profession, and for several years taught successfully in Alabama. Just before secession he moved to Tuskegee, and was there military instructor in the Collegiate Institute. His career as a teacher was brilliant and successful, while his genial disposition and engaging manners secured for him hosts of friends and admirers wherever he lived. In May. 1861, soon after hostilities had actually begun, in conjunction with Captain R. F. Ligon, Hon. David Clopton, Colonel Nick Gachet, Captain George Jones, Captain John H. Echols, Prof. J. F. Park and others, he raised the "Macon Confederates," and on the 26th of that month left for Richmond, where his company was assigned to the 12th Alabama Regiment. While the battle of Manassas was raging, on the 21st of July, the regiment took the cars for the scene of action, but, as stated in another place in this sketch, owing to the treachery of the conductor or engineer of the train, did not reach the field until the battle was over. For weeks and months after, near Fairfax, Va., Lieutenant Keeling and his brother officers employed themselves drilling, disciplining and training their command for the duties and realities of war, and the company was conceded to be the best equipped, the best instructed and the promptest and most intelligent in the regiment. Lieutenant Reeling's previous experience in the army proved of great advantage to his men, and his excellent advice and instruction was often afterwards found to be of great benefit. He was tall and commanding in figure, with a lofty brow and piercing eyes. These, together with talents, energy and intense devotion to the success of the Confederate cause, promised a brilliant career as a soldier. In April, 1862, the 12th Alabama was reorganized, and Lieutenant Keeling was unanimously elected captain of his company. During the trying Yorktown campaign, and in the arduous retreat to Richmond, before McClellan's advancing hosts, he cheered and inspired his men by his self-sacrificing example. On the night of the 30th of May the 12th Alabama was on outpost duty in the vicinity of Seven Pines. It had been raining incessantly during the day and increased in violence towards night. The writer of this shared with Captain Keeling his couch, consisting of blankets spread on rails, under a blanket stretched over us, for protection from the torrent of descending rain. Never shall I forget that night, nor the conversation I held with my departed friend. He gave me a retrospect of his life, replete with many interesting incidents, and full of instruction and wholesome advice. But I noticed that a certain degree of sadness marked his discourse, different from his usual genial and happy manner. He spoke of the certainty of a great and decisive battle between the opposing armies, and of the probability of his being killed or severely wounded, and all my efforts to banish the impression from his mind were unavailing. This feeling was but the harbinger of the approaching end. In our comfort-less situation it was impossible to sleep, and early the next morning we arose ready for the daily routine of duties.

About ten o'clock an officer from Gen. Rodes' headquarters brought orders to Col. Jones to have white badges placed upon the arms of his men that they might distinguish each other in battle, and to prepare for immediate action. With alacrity each man donned his badge, inspected his cartridges, and carefully loaded his musket. Pretty soon after, the command "fall in" was given, and Col. Jones, riding quickly forward, told his men that he was about to lead them into action, and that he expected every man to do his duty, and win for himself and his regiment a name. The 6th Alabama, under Colonel (subsequently Lieutenant General) Gordon marched by us with orders to deploy as skirmishers, and the 12th Alabama, filed in next. Many hundreds of hearts in that command which beat high with hope, and exulted in the prospect of meeting the despised foe, before sunset were stilled in death. On we moved, over fences, through mud and water waist deep and almost impenetrable under growth, across fields and ditches and fallen trees, listening to the oft repeated command "forward! close up! keep together!" and forward we went rapidly, and with yells, facing minie balls, grape and shells, reckless of danger. The 12th Alabama crossed the abatis and breastworks within twenty feet of the 12 captured Napoleon guns of the enemy. Twenty-eight dead horses and scores of lifeless and disabled Yankees were in our pathway. We moved through the camp of Gen. Casey, near his headquarters, and drove the enemy to a second abatis and a line of heavier earthworks. Just as we reached the abatis the command "halt," "fire and load kneeling!" were given, and scarcely had the order been repeated along the line, when Capt. Keeling fell, but the field was won, and his name, with thousands of his brave comrades, is worthy to live in the hearts of his countrymen forever.

It is proper to state that the above tribute to my friend, much extended, was written by me in 1867, and published in the *Tuskegee News*, edited then by my old comrade, A. F Henderson.

In returning through the camp of the enemy I was handed from General Casey's tent a copy of *Casey's Tactics*, written by himself, with his autograph in it, and I have preserved the book to this day. The men supplied themselves with many articles found in these tents, but with the exception of the desiccated food and articles of clothing, they could make little use of the trophies secured.

Private John U. Ingram of my company was killed, a gentle, manly youth, 18 years old.

It would be wrong not to mention the capital city of Richmond and her patriotic people in connection with the battle of Seven Pines. Every house in the city, whether stately or humble, was open for the Confederate wounded. The floors of the parlors, halls and verandas were covered by them. Beautiful girls and graceful matrons handed fruit and food to the soldiers who were marching through the city to the support of their comrades, and then turned to minister, angelically to the wounded and dying within their doors. These devoted women were ready with unlimited sacrifice for the cause they held sacred.

List of Killed and Wounded of the Twelfth Alabama Regiment, Third Brigade, Commanded by Brigadier General R. E. Rodes, at Battle of Seven Pines.

Field and Staff — Killed — Colonel R. T. Jones, Sergeant Major Robinson.

Company A — Killed — Sergeant C. Romanser, Corporals David

Pajori, D. Holahan, Privates James (or Pat) Ward, George Sanford, T. McDermott, C. Sannier, J. Barribas — total 7.

Wounded — Corporal J. Hiter, Privates M. Gaynor, slightly; William Dickens, James Ryan, Samuel Loggee, John Monday, L. Dondero, Pat Lanaham, A. Knorr, Robert Seville, George Krebbs, all seriously; N. Rainey, Joseph Gambonie, both mortally — total 13.

Company B— Killed— Privates R. A. Mitchell, W. K. Blake, Epperson, J. D. Findlayson, Harman, C. Lipsey, J. Massengale, J. C. Thomas, W B. Whitfield, J. T. Bice — total 10.

Wounded — J. Corby, Irwin, J. J. Smith, W. H. Veazey, all slightly; A. J. Gauron, A. Hollinshead, T. M. Kennedy, F. G. Little, F. J. Morgan, A. S. Martin, W. S. Phillips, A. G. Smith, H. C. Thomas, J. V. Wilkinson, all severely — total 14.

Company C — Killed — Privates J. D. Font, Thomas Pedue, F. Hullien, H. C. Reelen, B. Johnson — total 5.

Wounded — Sergeant Schermer, Corporal Husier, Privates Werneth R. Chapman, Siegel, Zundler, O'Brien, D. Rainey. M. Rainey. Y. Thompson, Stickney — total 9.

Companv D— Killed— Privates R. M. Dyap, W. M. Cardwell, Grimes, R. W. T. Horn, A. D. Matheney, Thomas Roads, J. F. Winslow, G. F. Brogden — total 8.

Wounded — Captain E. Tucker, Lieutenant J. T. Davis, Sergeant Horn, Corporals Horn and Bryant, Privates Cook, Cercy. G. W. Dyap, W F. Dvap, Lovvry, McNeal, Pritchett, E. L. Roads, Shudds, Strand, all slightly; J. M. Matheny, mortally — total 16.

Company E — Corporal Cunningham, Privates Bardis, Joseph Coffee, W. H. Crow, James Moore, B. F. Murrill, A. G. Roberts- total 7.

Wounded— Sergeant Murphy, Corporal Edwards, Privates M. J. Austin, J. M. Burrette, W. C. Brandon, John Carmor, L. A. Dabbs, William Farmer, C. Hunter, J. Little, A. B. Rooks, James Singleton, B. O. Word, all slightly; Edmund Drake, F. P. Patterson, C. C. Proster, severely — total 20.

Company F— Killed— Captain R. H. Keeling, J. U. Ingram.

Wounded— Privates R. F. Hall, J. R. Flewellen, B. F. Ingram, W. B. Ward, G. P. Ware, A. Wilkerson, F. S. Zachry, W. P. Zachry, slightly; M. A. Flournoy, mortally — total 9.

Company G — Killed — Lieutenant A. Hammond, Privates G. W. Kirkland, R. C. Bevil, H. I. Clifton, G. B. Packuss, J. S. Renfroe — total 6.

Wounded — Lieutenant J. M. Hardcastle, Privates M. Hawk, R. K. Crawley, E. S. Patten, all dangerously; Corporal Messier, J. M. Miller, M. Messier, William Steward, J. Derrick, J. Sisk, J. Stephens, I. Perkins, slightly; T. W. Keys, T. J. Rogers, J. J. Atchley, severely — total 16.

Company H — Killed — Captain J. H. Darwin, Lieutenant E. Ryan, Corporal Hefly, Privates S. E. Blankenship, M. F. Dement, Thomas Dunn, W R. Harris, J. J. McAnear, E. A. Mabry, S. D. Priddy, Jordan Wake, A. Smith. Total, 12.

Wounded — Corporal Hamilton, severely; Privates E. J. Brown, mortally; J. C. Fowler, J. C. McCain, W. Renner, seriously; J. H. Burk, C. Higdon, J. L. Jenkins, A. J. Rufles; A. Roper, C. B. Cyan, slightly. Total, 11.

Company I — Killed — Privates W. Wooten, E. Carey, J. Tash. Total, 3.

Wounded — Lieutenant J. J. Nicholson, Corporals T. M. Shelton, G. A. Nelson, slightly; Privates James Burns, Feltach, R. Overstreet, L. O. Thomas, W Thomas, F. Trice, H. N. Waters, slightly; William Williams, A. Wooten, both badly. Total, 12.

Company K— Killed— Private J. M. C. Payne.

Wounded — Lieutenant Townsend, Lieutenant Fitzgerald, Sergeants Jones, Taylor, Ethridge, all mortally; Corporal Scott, Privates Abercrombie, W. S. Ford, N. H. Goslin, C. H. Herring, H. H. Rowell, W. Stallmarks, slightly; S. M. Adams, D. T Jenkins, J. A. Powell, all mortally. Total, 14.

H. A. Whiting,
A. A. A. General, 3rd Brigade, 3rd Division.

SUMMARY.

	KILLED.		WOUNDED.	
	Staff Officers.	Enlisted Men.	Officers.	Enlisted Men
12th Miss. Regt.	5	35	2	138
6th Ala.	11	91	18	264
5th Ala.	1	26	9	159
12th Ala.	5	55	6	133
4th Va. Batal'n	3	17	2	67
King Wm. Artil'y	1	1	1	22
Total	26	225	38	783

Aggregate loss in killed and wounded, 1,083. The brigade went into action with about 2,400 men and officers.

H. A. Whiting,
A. A. A. Gen. 3rd Brigade, 3rd Division.

General Robert E. Lee

The Seven Days Battle Around Richmond.

The latter part of June, 1862, was an eventful period in the history of the 12th Alabama and of the Army of Northern Virginia. While General Lee's army confronted McClellan's hosts before Richmond, Stonewall Jackson was in the Valley fighting a series of battles.

On the 26th of June the Confederate army was engaged with McClellan at Mechanicsville, which is near the Confederate capital. Our army suffered severely in this fight. On the 27th my regiment, brigade and division, under General D. H. Hill, took part in the battle of Gaines' Mill, near Cold Harbor, which proved to be one of the most hotly contested battles in which we were ever engaged. The enemy was commanded by General Porter. They had long lines of infantry, in double column, and numerous batteries of artillery, on top of a hill. It became our duty to cross a creek in a swamp, and the enemy had cut the timber so as to impede the advance of our attacking force. I can never forget that when in a short distance of the enemy we made a halt and I was placed in command of a detachment of four men from each company, and ordered to deploy in their front, and shoot the cannoneers who were doing fatal damage in our ranks. The cannon belched forth fire and smoke, and bursting shells were hurtling among us. Wounded men were being carried to the rear, while we were saddened by the sight of motionless and lifeless comrades. In obedience to instructions, I hurried forward through the lowland, and before we had gone two hundred yards we captured seven prisoners, and I disarmed and hurried them to the rear. One of my men volunteered to take charge of and carry them back, but I replied that he would be needed in the other direction, and left them to surrender themselves to the main body.

Sergeant Patton of Company I, a native of Portland, Maine, a volunteer in a Mobile company, kept near me and showed great gallantry. We marched as best we could in line till we reached a deep sunken road, near enough to one of the batteries to shoot the artillerymen. The men were not slow in doing execution, and very soon we silenced the battery in our immediate front. Before we did so they turned their shot and shell, grape and canister directly upon my small squad, and the limbs of trees and countless leaves fell upon us, cut down by the enemy's fire. During a cessation in the firing Sergeant Patton obtained my permission to go up a ravine in front and discover what was going on. In a short time he returned, leading a horse, with a splendid saddle and holster of pistols upon it, and a young Federal soldier walking by his side. Bringing him to me we searched the young man and found a dispatch in cipher from General Kearney to General McClellan. We could not read it, and I sent the horse and its rider with the dispatch to Colonel Gayle, who took the horse and his accouterments, including the holster of pistols, and sent the dispatch to General D. H. Hill. The Richmond papers next day gave an account of the capture, and stated that the dispatch was important, giving valuable information, and mentioned that it had been brought in by a Lieutenant of the 12th Alabama Regiment.

Noticing the great and prolonged quiet in front of us, I ordered my men to crouch low and proceed beyond the woods into an open field, and there, to our intense surprise, we found a long array, in one line, of knapsacks, haversacks, guns and cartridge boxes. I quickly found, by an examination of the baggage, that they belonged to the 20th Mass. Regt., and we begun to open the knapsacks, which contained, besides clothing, numerous letters from relatives and sweethearts, and many pictures of women. From these I was handed by one of the men a half dozen razors, one of which I now daily use, and a number of red silk sashes, which evidently belonged to officers. Also a number of ambrotypes, which I saved, and, the first opportunity, expressed to my home folks at La Grange, Georgia, near where my mother lived. I am sorry to relate that some of the letters, which were read aloud by the men after we returned to camp, were too obscene and improper to be written, and certainly should never have been preserved. We saw many artillery horses lying dead, and numerous cannoners by their side, stiff and cold. My little band remained in possession of the large collection of knapsacks, haversacks, etc., until recalled about night, and every man returned to his company loaded with trophies, many of them of some value, others worthless, except as curiosities. When the battle ended it was dark.

The next day, an extremely hot one, while we were in line of battle in the blazing sun, I witnessed a piece of recklessness, or, heroism, if you choose to call it so, on the part of Captain L'Etondal, of Company A, from Mobile. The Twelfth Alabama was stretched out, and the men were lying prone upon the ground, enduring the sun's rays, and suffering greatly from the heat. Suddenly their attention was drawn to a novel sight, perhaps never a similar one was seen in any battle. At the end of Company A an umbrella was stretched over the prostrate form of Captain Jules L'Etondal. Soon the notice of the enemy's artillery was attracted by the umbrella, and they began aiming their Napoleon guns at that portion of the regiment, and the balls began to strike in dangerous proximity to it, and to the brave men near it. The men of the other companies began to call aloud, "shut down that umbrella," "close it up, you old fool." The cries had no influence upon L'Etondal, or his company, and when, some of the other companies, indignant at his willingness to expose his comrades to the fire of the enemy, by his efforts to protect himself from the blazing rays of the burning sun, called to him that they would come and shut up the umbrella if he didn't do it, and a few rose and started toward the captain as if to carry out their threat, some of his company rose to meet them, and swore that he should keep the umbrella raised over head, if he wanted to, and it was none of their d_ _d business. This state of affairs continued for some little time, but L'Etondal kept up his shade, and was totally oblivious to the commands and entreaties of the men, and his own company humored him, laughing at his persistence. When we were ordered to move forward, the captain, with his two hundred and fifty pounds of avoirdupois, streaming with perspiration, continued to hold aloft his umbrella.

During the time we were in this recumbent position, our division commander, General D. H. Hill and his staff rode by, and I witnessed in him a truly remarkable instance of his characteristic will which seemed to dominate physical pain, and in performance of duty made him regardless of self-sacrifice. One of the enemy's shells burst in front of the passing horsemen, and a piece of it cut under the arm of General Hill, tore away a portion of his uniform, his vest, if he had on any, and his shirt, and left a portion of the bare flesh on his side exposed. Wonderful to relate, the countenance of the General was unchanged, so far as we could see. No remark was made about the piece of shell, nor the work it had done, and no change was apparent in the gait of the horses, or at all in the conduct of General Hill or his comrades. This exhibition of indifference reminded me of seeing, during the seven days battles, while passing along a road, Stonewall Jackson* and D. H. Hill, who were brothers-in-law, dismount from their horses, and, sitting on a rail fence, pour syrup from a small bottle upon biscuits, which they were eating, passing the syrup to each other as they ate. During the time shell and shot were falling thick and fast around them, but they did not seem to hear them, not to be at all concerned about their safety. Such wonderful presence of mind had an encouraging influence over the weary and worn infantrymen as they trudged by, moving toward the enemy and witnessing an occasional comrade fall wounded and carried to the rear.

Winter at Hamilton's Crossing.

Our regiment, after being under heavy fire on the 13th and 14th of December, 1862, at Fredericksburg, supporting General Maxcy Gregg's South Carolinians, and witnessing the terrific slaughter of the Yankees on the day first mentioned, after marching and counter marching, located under tents at Hamilton's Crossing.

This regiment was in command of Colonel S. B. Pickens, with L. Gayle as adjutant, J. C. Goodgame, lieutenant colonel, and A. Proskauer as major, J. L. Walthall, late of Company I was quartermaster, and A. T. Preston, of Woodvilie North Alabama, commissary. After we had been in camp about a week, while standing around the camp fires, waiting for the announcement of supper, the colonel's orderly, Jack Mallory, brought me an order as follows:

"Headquarters 12th Ala. Regiment, January 3rd, 1863.

"First Lieut. R. E. Park of Co. F, will report for duty as Acting A. Q. M. of the 12th Ala. Regiment.

(Signed) "S. B. Pickens, Col. Comdg. , "L. Gayle, Adjutant."

This order was a great surprise to me, and not a welcome one, but, yielding to the persuasion of Captain McNeely and others, who thought it a compliment, I reported to Regimental Headquarters, where I told the colonel that I had little acquaintance with business affairs, having left college to join the army, and I feared my ability to properly perform the duties of the office. He laughed at my objections, and told me that he had thought over the names of a number, and had finally decided that I was the proper officer to take the place of the quartermaster, who had left the regiment, and was then absent without leave. My instructions were to report to the wagon yard, take charge of the wagons with the horses and mules, teamsters, and such

---

*The editor who served in the command of General Jackson saw him on more than one occasion evince similar imperturbability, whilst minie balls rained around and shells exploded with terrific sound and results near him — he sat firmly in his saddle on "Old Sorrel" smiling grimly, as those a-foot about him bent, in his estimation, idly, to avoid preordained fate.

baggage as I might find. I had further orders to arrest the absent quartermaster, if he should present himself. This last I had no occasion to do, as he never reported to the regiment again. The colonel left me one of his bay horses, "Pintail" by name, and the next morning, when I visited the regiment, I was saluted by many humorous remarks, was asked "if my head didn't swim," "please don't ride over me, mister," "I wish *I* could ride," "wish *I* had a bomb-proof job," ect., etc. By laughing good-humoredly at these sallies, they quickly discontinued their attempts at wit at my expense.

I found an excellent Virginia negro named Jim who had been acting as cook for Captain W., and I promptly employed him, and retained William McKinney of Company B as wagon master, William Howell as quartermaster sergeant, and Potter as clerk.

After the receipt of a small supply of clothing and shoes and distributing the same to the ragged and shoeless of the regiment I found that my clerk was charged with selling some of the articles, and I reported him to headquarters. He wept and attempted to explain the deficiency, and to my surprise, next day, he received an order directing him to report to Brigade Quartermaster J. C. Bryan, as his clerk. I parted with him without regret, and was greatly annoyed by his refusing to receive my requisitions as they were made out, and which I had Captain Brown, quartermaster of the Third Alabama to overlook and pronounce correct. After they were sent to me, I would return them without the crossing of a "t," or the dotting of an "i," in the original form, and they were always accepted. In February an order was received to send my cook to the brigade quartermaster's camp, and, jumping upon "Pintail," I galloped to General Rodes' headquarters at Grace Church, and walking rapidly down the aisle to the altar, handed the order to the general and asked him politely, but excitedly, what the order meant. He read it and said he never saw it before, and inquired of Major Whiting and other staff officers what they knew about it. Major Whiting replied that it was issued at the request of Major Bryan, who said the negro was a regular teamster. This I positively denied, and stated that he had never been reported as such by me, and was my cook, and that the brigade quartermaster wished to avail himself of his services, not as a teamster, but as his personal cook. The general then said, "the matter is between you and Major Bryan, I will have nothing to do with it." I thanked him for his decision and rode rapidly back to my tent, and told Jim to remain as cook, much to his delight.

Sketch of the Twelfth Alabama

The brigade quartermaster and his clerk subjected me to a great many little annoyances, but I gave satisfaction to the Colonel commanding my regiment, and to the officers and men. Many long rides were taken to Hanover Junction, to Fredericksburg, and to other points after hay and oats for the horses, as well as for articles shipped for the use of the men, mainly clothing and shoes, with which they were illy supplied.

In company with Major Gordon of the 6th Alabama, and brother of Gen. John B. Gordon, and Capt. J W McNeely, of my company, I frequently made visits to the charming young ladies living near our camp. The Misses Lawrence, Parrish, Withers and others were all of them musical ladies and gracious and hospitable.

The latter part of April we broke camp, and on the 1st of May General Hooker crossed the Rappahannock between Fredericksburg, and Spotsylsvania, near Chancellorsville, and on the third the great battle by that name was fought, and, the idol of the army, General Lee's right arm, Stonewall Jackson, was killed by mistake by a detachment from a North Carolina regiment. This battle was, without doubt, one of the grandest strategic movements that the world has ever known. This was the only battle of importance that I missed, up to my capture at Winchester, except the battle of Sharpsburg, in which my company and regiment were engaged.

The quarter-masters, with their teamsters and wagons, were located near Hamilton's Crossing, and information was received from General Stuart that we might expect to be attacked by the enemy's cavalry. The men were all assembled, and, by order of the division quarter-master, Major Harmon, I was placed in command of the little group, composed of quartermasters, wagon masters, cooks and stragglers, all of whom I armed from the ordnance stores, and had them to load their guns, and gave them directions how to meet the cavalry when they approached. I had the wagons parked in a square, with the horses and men within the square, and the guns were stacked and ready for use, one man being on guard to each wagon and on the lookout. Fortunately, the cavalry did not attack us, as it was very probable my entire crowd, composed of about ninety men, would have fled without delay, upon hearing the first gun. This great battle was the cause of the death of many brave and promising offices and men in my regiment. Captain McNeely, my most intimate friend and mess-mate for the past two years, had the calf of his leg penetrated by a grape shot, and was disabled for the rest of the service. He spent the remainder of the war at Talladega, drilling conscripts.

Private P. W. Chappell, of Company F, was shot entirely through the body by a minie ball, but, in less then sixty days, reported again for duty.

An immense number of prisoners were crowded into the cars and shipped from Hamilton's and Guinea's to Richmond. Some of these prisoners were rude; boisterous and violent. Many of them were foreigners whose language we did not understand. All seemed to know how to use oaths, and to indulge in profanity profusely.

In the various battles, which we have fought to this time, we have had with us Carter's famous Virginia Battery of artillery, commanded first by Captain, now Colonel Thomas H. Carter, and lastly by his brother, Captain William Page Carter, now of Boyce, Virginia.

These were trained and gallant officers and their men were superb soldiers. Carter's Battery ranked deservedly among the famous artillery companies of the Confederate Army, and Battle's Brigade always felt better when they were in proximity to these patriotic Virginians.

We remained encamped near Grace Church the remainder of the winter and until May, 1863. During the time the tedium of camp life was seldom broken.

Rev. W. A. Moore, an old college classmate at Auburn, flattered me by getting a transfer from the Sixty-first Georgia regiment to my company, and favored us on Sundays with good sermons.

Rev. (Captain) Tom W Harris, of the Twelfth Georgia regiment, an old college-mate, preached for us several Sundays, and a Baptist preacher, a substitute in my company, Rev. E. J. Rogers, also gave us religious services.

Rev. W. J. Hoge, D. D., who had left his church in New York, preached at Grace Church to an immense crowd. Later, he preached the funeral sermon of Stonewall Jackson, and his pathos and eloquence brought blinding tears to the eyes of many an old soldier, unused to weep.

Soon after the battle of Chancellorsville, at the request of all the company, and in compliance with my own wishes, I declined to remain as quartermaster, and asked to be returned to my company. There was at that time no commissioned officer, and I valued highly the unanimous wish and request of my comrades to resume the command.

Our regiment, during its entire career, was favored with two faithful chaplains, one, Rev. Mark. S. Andrews, D. D., a graduate of

Emory College, Georgia, and a prominent Alabama minister, living at Tuskegee, served until the second year of the war. I wished to have my old school fellow, W. A. Moore, selected as his successor, but Colonel Pickens gave the appointment to Rev. Henry D. Moore, D. D., a graduate of Citadel Academy at Charleston. Both of these have died since the war, after careers of usefulness and honor. Dr. Moore was with us during the years 1863 and part of 1864. He organized a Christian association in our regiment, the only pledge to be taken by its members being that they should not indulge in intoxicating drinks nor in profanity. Through his influence some very profane men stopped the silly and undignified habit. Among the leading soldiers who joined were, Colonel Pickens, Dr. George Whitfield, Captain Davis of Company D, and others.

A Brigade Association was also formed with General C. A. Battle as president, Maj. R. H. Powell, of the 3rd Alabama, as vice president, and myself as secretary, and we were favored with addresses by a number of distinguished ministers. Among them I recall Rev. Dr. L. Rosser, Methodist; Rev. Dr. J. L. Burrows, a Baptist, who after the battle of Seven Pines, spent the night going over the battlefield and relieving the necessities of many wounded Confederate soldiers, notably of the 12th Alabama. Rev W. C. Powell, a chaplain of the 14th North Carolina, often visited the regiment, and was always welcome. The regiment and brigade were certainly blessed in the presence and visits of these good and faithful men of God. They were men of ability and did noble service in their holy calling.

I give the following brief sketch of Dr. Andrews. Rev. Mark S. Andrews was born February 23, 1826, in Oglethorpe county. Ga., and died May 14, 1898, in Mobile, Ala. His parents moved to Alabama and settled near Oak Bowery. He completed his college course at Oxford, Ga. In 1832 he became a member of the Alabama Conference, M. E. Church, South. He taught in Tuskegee Female College in its infancy with Dr. A. A. Lipscomb and Dr. G. W. F. Price. In 1861, as a member of the 12th Alabama regiment in Captain Ligon's company, F, he went to Virginia. At this time disease ravaged and destroyed its soldiers, and he counted his life as nothing when ministering to the sick and dying by day and night. A choice sense of humor gave him pleasant variety in social life. He was a man of integrity, gentle and steadfast, who overcame enemies and attached friends.

January 29, 1863 — A committee consisting of Captains Fischer, Hewlett and Ross were appointed to invite the officers of Battle's brigade to assemble at the headquarters of the 12th Alabama and take into consideration the propriety of memorializing Congress on the subject of regimental and company re-organization, tomorrow at 9 o'clock. There is a great desire on the part of many to enjoy the benefits of re-organization. Many privates hope to be elected officers and many officers expect to secure promotions.

January 30. — At 9 o'clock the line officers of the 6th Alabama met those of the 12th Alabama at our camp and appointed a committee of three from each regiment to draft a memorial to be presented to Congress. Captain Bowie of the 6th and I were chosen to visit the officers of the 3rd and 5th Alabama and notify them to meet us at six o'clock, and participate in our proceedings. At six o'clock the meeting was called to order, Capt. Bowie being chairman and Lieutenant Dunlap, of the 3rd Alabama, acting as secretary. The memorial drafted was read and discussed, pro and con, by Captains Bowie and Bilbro and Lieutenants Larey, Dunlap and Wimberly, and the meeting adjourned to meet Monday at 3 o'clock.

The meeting was held, a memorial adopted and a committee appointed to get signatures to the petition and forward it to Hon. Robert Jemison, Jr., C. S. Senator, and Hon. W. P Chilton, representative from Alabama, for presentation to the Confederate Congress.

February 3. — Orders came at night to be ready to move to Hanover Junction at 6 o'clock. Battle's Alabama brigade left winter quarters at 6 and a half o'clock for Gordonsville and arrived there at 2 P M. We took the cars at midnight for Hanover Junction. General R. D. Johnston's North Carolina brigade preceded ours.

February 7. — Our brigade took the train for Richmond early in the morning and reached the capital at 2 o clock, formed in the city, and marched to music to the outer fortifications on York river railroad, about four miles from the city.

February 8. — Went to Richmond and visited the Hall of the House of Representatives and heard eulogies pronounced over the dead body of Col. J. J. Wilcox, of Texas. At night I saw *Virginia Cavalier* played at Richmond Theatre. R. D'Orsay Ogden, manager, J. W. Thorpe, former drum-major of the Twelfth Alabama, J. Wilkes Booth, Harry McCarthy, W H. Crisp, Theodore Hamilton, John Templeton, and Alice Vane are the favorite actors. Soldiers are not critics, but are ever ready to be amused.

I remained in the city all day, meeting with many officers and men at the hospitals, the Exchange Hotel and Ballard House, and Spotswood Hotel. At night saw *Lady of the Lake* acted. At its conclusion, en route to camp, stopped with Captain Hewlett and Lieutenant J. M. Tate of the Third Alabama at a "shindig" and had an enjoyable time. Kissing games were popular, and some of the dancers were "high kickers," but not over graceful. Late in the afternoon the brigade moved three miles further to the front, to meet the expected expedition of "Beast" Butler, who was located somewhere near Drury's Bluff on the James. The "Beast" has been outlawed by President Davis and is generally detested. He should keep, as heretofore, to the rear, and avoid capture.

Colonel W. G. Swanson's Sixty-first Alabama regiment joined our brigade, and the Twenty-sixth Alabama, Colonel E. A. O'Neal, was transferred to Mobile. Colonel C. A. Battle had been promoted brigadier-general and placed in command of Rodes' brigade. As there were only nine companies in the Sixty-first, the Secretary of War declined to issue a commission as colonel to Colonel Swanson, and he returned to Alabama. I was glad to greet the Sixty-first, because among its officers were some intimate friends of mine. Among these were Captain J. W. Fannin and his brother, Lieutenant A. B. Fannin, Captain S. B. Paine and his son, Lieutenant Hendree Paine, Captain E. F. Baber and First Lieutenant Edward P. Hendree, Captain B. F. Howard and Lieut. C. C. Long. All of these from Tuskegee, the place from which my company was enlisted. These officers are all good men and true.

February 15. A light snow covered mother earth's bosom today and kept us from the city. Our trips to the city are greatly enjoyed, and all are allowed to go there as often and stay as long as they please. There is a joke in camp in regard to Jim Lester exchanging a jug of water for one of whiskey in a city barroom. He did it as adroitly as Simon Suggs could have done.

February 18. Rode on the tender of an engine to Orange C. H. Paid $6.00 for breakfast, and walked to our old camp.

February 22. Washington's birthday The great Virginian doubtless looks down approvingly upon the course of his successors, Lee, Johnston, Stuart, A. P. Hill, Rodes and others. Lee and Jackson excel the great father of his country as soldiers.

February 26. Hired Charles, negro servant of private Kimbrough, for one year, at $25.00 per month. Charles is a good cook and forager.

At night I attended a grand ball at Dr Terrell's, to which I contributed $25.00. General Ramseur and his pretty bride, nee Miss Richmond, of North Carolina, were present. Pretty women, and officers in Confederate grav, were an inspiring sight. Mrs. Carter, formerly Miss Taliaferro (since Mrs. John H. Lamar, and Mrs. Harry Day of Georgia), was one of the brightest belles.

While in camp, near Fredericksburg, I obtained a week's furlough to visit Richmond, and went there with Dr. George Whitfield, our beloved surgeon. Stopped at Hatton's on Mayo Street. Escorted Miss Ella H. to Miss Nannie King's marriage. At night Dr. Whitfield and I went to the "Varieties" and saw *Naval Engagements*, and *The Married Rake*. Harry McCarthy was the leading actor.

Sunday, April 19. A glorious beautiful spring day. Private W. A. Moore of my company, preached an excellent sermon on the 8th verse, 2nd chapter of Ephesians. Private Rogers of my company preached in the afternoon. Received a letter announcing the marriage of my brother James F. Park to Miss Emma Bailey of Tuskegee, and wrote a congratulatory letter.

April 25. Rev. F. M. Kennedy, a North Carolina Chaplain, preached at Round Oak Church. It was an able sermon. General Wm. N. Pendleton had been expected, but failed to come.

April 28. One year ago the "Macon Confederates," Company F, were re-organized while stationed at Yorktown. R. H. Keeling, J. W. McNeeley and I were respectively elected captain, first and second lieutenants by a unanimous vote. It was the turning point in my life. The life of a private soldier is not an enviable one, and I intend to do what I can to relieve and cheer the brave men who have, by their votes, promoted me from their ranks. Our former captain, R. F. Ligon, and Lieutenants George Jones and Zuber returned to Alabama.

April 29. This day, twelve months ago, I was assigned to duty as second-lieutenant in the "provisional army of the Confederate States." Today we are hurriedly notified that General Hooker, the successor of the unsuccessful Burnside, has effected a landing near Fredericksburg, and Rodes' old brigade, under Colonel O'Neal of the Twenty-sixth Alabama, is ordered to meet them. My, duties, as acting quartermaster, require me to have several wagons loaded with officers' baggage, quartermasters stores, tents, etc., and driven to Hamilton's Crossing, where we remained all night.

April 30. Our brigade moved to the opposite side of the Richmond, Fredericksbnrg and Potomac Railroad, and drew up in line of battle, while our wagon train moved a mile and remained until 12 o'clock midnight, and then moved to Guinea's station.

Battle of Chancellorsville.

May 2. Rested until night, when we were ordered to move as rapidly as possible our trains to Bowling Green. Today the great battle of Chancellorsville began, and Rode's old brigade of Alabamians charged the Yankees brilliantly, driving them out of their newly erected breastworks thrice in succession, and capturing three batteries with horses and equipments entire attached.

Captain McNeely of Company F, was severely wounded in right leg, below the knee, by a grape shot tearing a hole through the flesh. Privates Chappell and Henderson were wounded in the arm. Chappell was engaged in a close, hand to hand encounter when injured. Poor Ben was carried, at the point of the bayonet, into the engagement, complaining all the while of being sick, but he only had what we called "battlefield colic," and was forced into the thickest of the fray, where he received a bullet in one of his arms, and from the wound lost the arm and spent the remainder of the war at home. The day's fight was a grand success for our arms. Our wagon train was moving all night to escape Stoneman's Yankee cavalry, which was reported as ravaging the country, after having taken Marye's Heights, and to be now in search of our train. We passed a fevy miles beyond Bowling Green.

May 3. The great battle continued today. Rodes' Brigade, to quote that officer's language, "covered itself with glory." Generals Jackson and Stuart complimented it. Rodes was made a full Major General, and after the distressing news of Stonewall Jackson's wound, became senior officer of the field under Lee. He was in actual command of the army next to Lee, but his modesty caused him to turn over the command to Gen. J. E. B. Stuart of the cavalry, one of the most dashing officers I ever saw. In F Company, Capt. McNeely, Joe Black, Tom Foulk, Jim Lester, West Moore, Fletch Zachry and Sergt. Simmons were wounded. The 12th Alabama lost four captains and three lieutenants, among them Capt. H. W. Cox, and Lieut. Dudley. We lost a total of 134 men out of our small regiment, in killed, wounded and missing. Thirteen were killed outright and 87 wounded severely. The brigade lost five field officers. Lieut. Col. A. M. (Gordon, brother of Gen. John B. Gordon, was killed. He was a line officer and a true Christian.

Alter being shot lie he calmly said he was willing to die for the cause. "Fighting Joe's" army was terribly repulsed, and forced to retreat beyond the Rappahannock.

The enemy's cavalry contented itself with tearing up a part of the railroad track and cutting telegraph wires, thus interrupting communication with Richmond.

May 5. There are 6,000 prisoners of war at Guinea's and others coming in hourly. Among them is Brigadier General Hayes, said to be a renegade native of Richmond. The prisoners were boisterous, impertinent and insulting in their conversation. A great rain storm fell and they were in great discomfort. I pity them. There are numerous foreigners among them, Germans, Swiss, Italians, Irish, *et alios*. Our help from such quarters is *nil*.

May 6. After the battle my regiment and train returned to our former camp. Everything and everybody seemed changed, sad and dejected. I greatly miss my dear friend, Captain McNeely. He was my most intimate associate and I love him as a brother. He is a graduate of the La Grange College at Florence, Ala., and taught for a while with Professor W. F. Slaton at Auburn, and, more recently, at the Military School at Tuskegee, with Captain Keeling. He is a fine scholar, a very amiable man, and popular with the company

I am performing double duty, acting as quarter master of the regiment and in command of my company. I have repeatedly asked Colonel Pickens to relieve me from the former, but he has not consented to do so. My men urge me to return to them.

May 10. A beautiful Sabbath, recommended by General Lee as a day of thanksgiving and prayer for our recent great victory Strange to say "Fighting Joe" Hooker issued a proclamation to his army after they had retreated across the river, congratulating them upon their great victory. How could General Lee and General Hooker both be victorious? I helped to bury Captain Cox of Company B, Twelfth Alabama, at Grace Church this afternoon. He was a gallant officer.

May 12. News of the death of General Jackson, the true hero of the war, fills the whole army with grief. He resembled Napoleon in his methods more nearly than any of our generals. Truly Lee has lost his most reliable aid, and was correct in speaking of him as his "right arm." His name and his deeds are embalmed in our hearts. The regiment returned from picket, and I again solicited permission to return to my company and that another officer be detailed as quartermaster. Colonel Pickens replied that if his brother's commission did not arrive in three days he would relieve me.

May 14. Drilled my company for the first time in some months. Was stopped by a refreshing rain, which will cool the air and benefit our wounded. First Sergeant Hall was ordered, on account of his wound, to report to General Winder, and I promoted George Wright to his place.

May 15. Pay roll completed, inspected and approved by the Colonel. Commanded a division of two companies on battalion drill. Promised relief as acting quartermaster by Monday next. Company F was paid off for March and April, and the sutler's wagon will be well patronized for a few days. Ginger cakes, porous and poor, cost 25 cents each. Vegetables and fruits are out of reach of the privates.

May 18. Relieved as acting quarter master and returned to the command of my company. Receipted for and issued to the most needy among my men, thirteen pairs of pants, four jackets, nine pairs of socks, and several pairs of shoes. Captain J. Miles Pickens, a brother of the Colonel, is now quartermaster.

May 19 and 20. Drilled company in breaking files to the rear, breaking in platoons, loading by numbers and stacking arms. The men have grown rusty The election, held to decide who of the company should wear the "Badge of Honor" for gallantry at Chancellorsville, resulted in twelve votes each for Sergeant Wright and Private Chappell. In drawing the latter won, and his name was sent to General Lee.

May 24. Heard Rev. Dr. Moses D. Hoge preach a fine sermon at Camp Alabama. Lieutenant Wright came and reported the loss of a pair of new boots and a number of new novels sent me. I am nearly barefooted and wanted something to read, so my regret may be imagined.

May 29. Grand review of Rodes' Division by Generals R. E. Lee, A. P. Hill and R. E. Rodes. The day was warm and we marched three miles to the reviewing grounds, and stood several hours before getting properly aligned. After preparing for review and passing in review before General Rodes, General Lee arrived and went through the same movements before him. I commanded the fourth division of the regiment.

June 4. Regan a tramp through Valley of Virginia to Maryland, and marched about 18 miles, halting near Spotsylvania C. H. June 5,

6, 7 and 8. On the march to Culpeper C. H., where we stayed a day supporting Stuart's cavalry, while he drove back some raiders near Brandy Station.

June 9 to 18. On the road to Maryland. Captured Berryville, Bunker Hill and Martinsburg.

Advance Into Maryland and Pennsylvania.

June 19. Crossed the Potomac by wading at Williamsport, Md. and marched through Hagerstown. A majority of the people seem to be unionists, though there are some delightful exceptions. Bivouacked at Funkstown. Dined at Mr. Syester's, a good Southerner. Gave 75 cents in Confederate money for a pound of stick candy.

June 20. With Captain Hewlett and Lieutenant Oscar Smith, of Third Alabama, called on Misses Mary Jane and Lizzie Kellar, young ladies just from a Pennsylvania female college, and heard them play and sing Southern songs. This was a very agreeable surprise to us all.

June 21. Attended Divine services at Methodist Episcopal Church in Hagerstown. At tea met Miss Rose Shafer, and found her to be a brave Belle Boyd in her words and acts. She is a true blue Southerner.

June 22. Took up line of march to Pennsylvania, and passed through Hagerstown in columns of companies. Crossed Pennsylvania line near Middleburg and camped at Greencastle.

June 23. Lieut. J. W. Wright's resignation was accepted, and Sergt. G. W. Wright was elected in his stead. I appointed T. H. Clower, First Sergt., and Corp. Bob Stafford a Sergeant.

June 24. Marched to Harrisburg and passed through Marion and Chambersburg. We see many women and children, but few men. General Lee has issued orders prohibiting all misconduct or lawlessness, and urging the utmost forbearance and kindness to all. His address and admonition is in contrast with the conduct of the Northern Generals, who have invaded the South with their soldiers. But it is in accord with true civilization. We cannot afford to make war upon women and children and defenseless men.

June 25. Breakfasted with a citizen who refused all pay, though I assured him Confederate money would soon take the place of greenbacks.

June 26. Marched through Greenvillage and Shippensburg. It rained all day. Had a nice bed of dry wheat straw at night, and slept soundly, undisturbed by dreams or alarms.

June 27. Marched through several small towns, and two miles beyond Carlisle, on the Baltimore turnpike, at least 25 miles. Ate an excellent supper at Mr. A. Spott's.

June 28. Breakfasted with some brother officers at Mr. Lee's. His daughters waited upon the tables, and we were served with hot rolls and waffles, butter and honey. Fried chicken also graced the table, and, I need not say, everything was hugely enjoyed. I went to an Episcopal Church in Carlisle, and, after the close of the service, was passing some well dressed ladies, to whom I lifted my hat, when one of them spoke to me kindly and inquired what State I was from, and upon reply told me that their minister was from Florence, Alabama. She spoke very gently and without a word of abuse, or reproof, or remonstrance. I went alone to the National Hotel for dinner. Found an unfriendly and scowling crowd of rough looking men in the office, but I walked up to the desk and registered and called for dinner. I was late and the dinner was quite a poor one, and was rather ungraciously served by a plump, Dutchy looking young waitress. I paid for it in Confederate money.

June 29. Crossed Blue Ridge Mountains at a gap at Papertown, where many of our men obtained a supply of writing paper. Marched on turnpike to Petersburg and took the Frederick City road, bivouacking at Heidlersberg.

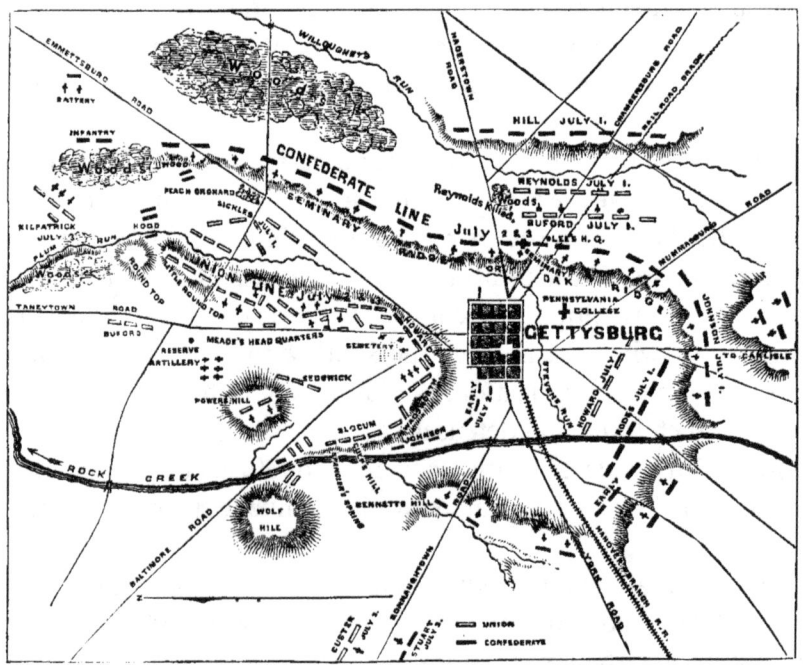

Battle of Gettysburg.

July 1. Marched through Middletown towards Gettysburg. This proved to be one of the most eventful days of my life. We could hear and see the shelling in front of Gettysburg, and were soon in range. Rodes' division was actively engaged in a very short time. His old Alabama brigade, under Colonel O'Neal, was shelled fiercely. Captain James T. Davis of Company D was killed near me. Another shell exploded in my company and wounded Corporal J. H. Eason and Private Lucius Williams, while we halted in a hilly woods. We passed the woods and a wheat field, where private Rogers, our Baptist preacher, had his knee shattered by a minie ball. We continued to advance and soon made a charge upon the enemy not far from the Seminary. We ran them some distance and halted. There Lieutenant Wright was wounded in the head, by my side. I spoke to him and he calmly asked me to examine his wound, and tell him frankly whether I thought it would prove fatal. I looked at his bloody head, lifted the hair from over the wound and found his brain exposed, the bone on top of his head having been carried away. I answered him cheerfully and reassuringly, bidding him lie close to the ground until he could be removed. I gave him some water out of my canteen and made him lie down as low as possible, as the bullets were passing thick and fast by and over us, and often striking some one near by. Captain Hewlett and Private Lester were wounded near me. While urging my men to fire and keep cool, I received a ball in my hip. It was wonder, a miracle, I was not afterwards shot a half dozen times, but a merciful Providence preserved me. After long exposure to heavy fire from a superior force of the enemy, we were ordered to fall back to a stone fence. Captain J. J. Nicholson of Company I kindly offered to help me as I hobbled along, though I urged him to abandon me and save himself. Colonel Pickens sent me to hospital on Major Proskauer's horse. Our gallant Jew Major smoked his cigars calmly and coolly in the thickest of the fight. At the field hospital, an old barn, I was put in a tent with Captains Ross and Hewlett, Lieutenants Wright and Fletcher, Corporal Eason and Henry Lamar. Poor John Preskitt was mortally wounded. He died saying: "All is right." My company had all of its officers wounded and about half of its men. Every officer, except Captain Thomas, on the right wing of the regiment, was either killed or wounded. The brigade suffered severely. Our division drove the enemy through the town, capturing many prisoners, including nearly all of their wounded. Surgeon George Whitfield was kept very busy.

July 2. Limped inside the barn, saw Preskitt's body, and urged a decent burial by the ambulance corps. He leaves a very helpless family. Lieutenant Fletcher of Company G died by my side. Nine of my company were wounded yesterday. Pierce Ware returned to the company in time for the fight. Our forces fought Meade's command all day, and the cannonading was wonderfully distinct and terrific.

July 3. Heavy cannonading and musketry without cessation. Attempted to storm the heights, but failed. Stuart sent back a large number of captured wagons. Our anxiety for news was intense. We fear defeat in the enemy's country, but hope and pray for victory. We have every confidence in Lee and Stuart.

July 4. A memorable day! All able to walk were sent towards Maryland, and the badly wounded were hauled away. Dr. Whitfield was very kind and placed me in the first ambulance, driven by Sam Slaton, in company with Lieutenant Wright and Captains Ross and Hewlett. The night was a dark, dreary, rainy one. At 1 o'clock A. M. we started after a long halt on Fairfield road, towards Hagerstown, riding over an execrable mountain road. We were suffering, wet and anxious. The Yankee cavalry attacked our train and took several of our wagons, including the third one in our rear. They were firing uncomfortable near. Our ambulance broke down at this critical time, and we waked up a farmer, got his small market wagon, left one horse with him and drove the other, with his wagon, on to Hagerstown. Captain Pickens, quartermaster, aided us much. At Washington Hotel in Hagerstown, the proprietor gave us sandwiches and a bottle of whiskey and spoke cheerily.

July 5. We reached Williamsport, after a gloomy night, at 6 A. M., and drove our horse across the Potomac and reached Martinsburg at 2 P. M., had our wounds dressed, ate dinner in the hospital, drove four miles and spent the night at Mr. Stanley's.

July 6. Arrived at Winchester at 4 o'clock, turned over our horse and wagon to provost marshal, Captain Cullen, and left Winchester on mail coach, reaching Woodstock at 11 o'clock at night, and slept on the hotel floor. Citizens are anxious for news and asked many questions.

July 7. Breakfasted and left on stage for Staunton, eating dinner at Harrisonburg, where a generous stranger paid our bill. Money is not plentiful with us. Reached Staunton at 8:30 at night and stopped at American Hotel Hospital.

July 8. Drew a month's pay and obtained transfer to general hospital, Richmond. Captain H. and I hired a horse and buggy for $12.00 to carry us to Middle river, six miles distant, to get our valises from Captain Haralson, quartermaster.

July 9. Reached Richmond 5 P. M. Went to hospital number four, Dr. J. B. Reid. Dr. A. V. P. Garnett gave me a thirty day's furlough, approved by General Winder.

Camp Near Orange Courthouse August, 1863.

General Lee placed the Army of Northern Virginia in position at and around Orange Courthouse during the summer of 1863. At this time General Longstreet, with his corps, was sent to Georgia to the aid of General Bragg.

For some days our regiment and brigade remained quiet, and during the time the famous review by General Lee took place. The review was a very brilliant sight, with the magnificently dressed officers, for most of them did manage to keep new uniforms, and were in marked contrast to the poorly clad privates and line officers. The only field officer of the Twelfth Alabama present was Colonel Pickens. There was only one captain in camp, and I was senior first lieutenant, and third in rank. This illustrates the great severity with which the enemy's bullets and camp sickness had dealt with my regiment.

An amusing incident during this great review was the whistling by some of the men in perfect imitation of the partridge, or "Bob White." They used their lips in imitating the bird whenever Lieutenant and Acting A. G. Daniel Partridge, of General Battle's staff, rode by on his fine horse. The gallant officer was annoyed by this impertinence, on the part of the men, whom he could not possibly detect, and whom the company officers would not expose, but he was helpless and had to submit.

Sunday morning I was surprised by Adjutant Gayle coming to my tent and informing me that I was in command of the regiment, that Colonel Pickens had been sent for by General Rodes, and Captain Thomas had been detailed as brigade officer of the day, and that I, as the third officer in rank, was in command of the regiment, and that he awaited my orders. I directed him to draw up the regiment for regular Sunday inspection, and I recall, very distinctly, the hesitation and embarrassment that I felt in marching to the front of the regiment, then depleted to less than 300 men, and after the formation of the parade by the adjutant, giving the regiment a short drill in the manual of arms, and then breaking it into companies, and personally inspecting each gun in the command, as well as the cartridge-box and bayonet of each soldier. The arms of some of the companies were in most admirable condition, while others showed more or less rust and indifference on the part of the men who handled them.

It was a notable fact that there was not only not a field officer but not a single captain present during this parade, every company being commanded either by a lieutenant or a sergeant.

During our stay at this camp I had a visit from Gen. B. Graves of Tuskegee, whose son William, had been a member of the company, and had been arrested for desertion, and was then at headquarters under guard. The erect, dignified and courteous old gentleman, then probably 70 years of age, was grievously distressed by the conduct of his son, and anxious to prevent any severe punishment being inflicted upon him. One of the most eloquent letters that I ever read was handed to me by the father from the grieved mother. The trial did not take place, as soon after, when we resumed our march, he escaped and was never again seen in the Confederacy.

The beautiful wife of Col. Charles Forsyth, of the 3rd Alabama, visited the colonel in camp, and as she was a splendid horse-woman she attracted marked attention from the gallant young officers of the command.

I had the pleasure of forming the acquaintance of some charming families in that vicinity, among them the Misses Willis, Mrs. Goodwin and Miss Terrell, the two last daughters of the venerable Dr. Terrell, who lived to be over 90 years of age, and was a member of the Virginia Constitutional Convention after the close of the war.

I can never forget a brief conversation with General Rodes while at the depot at Orange C. H. on his return from a visit to Richmond. He told me of the appointment of General Battle to the command of the brigade, and stated that Colonel O'Neal of the Twenty-sixth Alabama, had asked for a transfer to the Western army. During the conversation General Rodes spoke most affectionately of my former captain, R. H. Keeling saying that he knew him at the Virginia Military Institute, and that he should have entered the army as a brigadier general instead of first lieutenant.

August 24. General R. E. Lee rode his famous horse, "Traveler," through our camp and near my tent. I lifted my hat and was saluted by our great commander. He is always greeted with cheers and acclamations when he passes near a regiment.

August 28 and 29. Colonel Battle received his commission as brigadier general, and at night was serenaded by a brass band from Doles' Georgia brigade. He responded in a very pretty speech.

September 4 and 5. An officer of the day Private Griffith of Company E, married a girl near Orange C. H. It is love in low life. He brought his *cara sposa* to see our encampment, and they were the observed of all observers.

September 14. The anniversary of my memorable skirmish near Boonsboro, (South Mountain) Md. We are ordered to Summerville Ford, near Rapidan Station, where the Yankees are threatening a passage. Marched very rapidly and halted a mile from the ford. Our artillery kept up a heavy firing for several hours and had several men killed. Captain Carter's battery cannot be excelled.

September 15 and 16. Rodes' division, composed of Daniel's and Ramseur's North Carolina, Doles' Georgia, and Battle's Alabama brigades, were marched out to witness a melancholy sight, the public shooting of one of Ramseur's brigade, who was convicted of desertion by a court martial and sentenced to be shot to death by musketry. It was a sad sight, but his death was necessary as a warning and lesson to his comrades. Each regiment was marched in front of the dead body, and his breast was pierced by several bullets. On return to camp we found two of my men, George Ward and Dick Noble, who had been on a scout across the river and captured a Yankee and carried him to General Rodes, and secured a splendid pistol and seven-shooting rifle. Heard Rev. Dr. L. Rosser deliver an eloquent lecture to our Christian Association on "patriotism, benevolence and religion."

Oct. 8, 1863. I drew from quartermaster Pickens, 15 envelopes, one quire of letter paper, half quire of note and half quire of foolscap paper and five pens. Such things are growing scarce, and show to what extremities we are rapidly approaching. Lieuts. F. A. Rogers and John R. Williams of Company A, were promoted Captain, and First Lieutenant of said company, and Lieutenant John Rogers of Company E, promoted to captain. At 3 P. M. we were ordered to pack up, and marched until 9 P. M. and camped near Dr. Terrell's, four miles from Orange C. H.

Oct. 9. At 4 o'clock A. M. we marched through Orange, waded Rapidan river, and bivouacked three miles from Madison C. H. Here our "spider wagon," as the North Carolina "Tar Heels" call our cooking utensil wagon, failed to come up and we had to "make up" our flour, water and salt on oil cloths, and bake before the fire on our gun ramrods, sticks, rails, etc. And, after salting our beef, hung it on poles before the fire until cooked. We were all hungry and ate heartily of our beef and bread.

Oct. 10. Continued our march through byroads and old fields, and new roads cut by the pioneer squads through the woods, until we came to the Sperryville turnpike, 11 miles from Culpeper C. H.

Oct. 11. We waded across Robinson river, as it is called, and occupied an old camp of the 6th Yankee army corps. It was on a high, bleak hill, where the wind blew constantly and fiercely, and rendered our sleep very uncomfortable. Such cold winds eighteen months ago, would have caused colds, coughs and pneumonia, but now we are accustomed to rough weather and thin clothing.

Battle of Warrenton Springs.

October 12. At 2 P M. we were aroused and started for the Rappahannock river. It was not a pleasure excursion. At 12 M. we came near the village of Jeffersonton, halted for a few minutes, and learned that a body of Yankee cavalry were in a church in the town, and General Battle was ordered to flank and capture the party if possible. The Third, Sixth and Twelfth Alabama regiments marched to the left, and the Fifth and Twenty-sixth Alabama to the right. After going about two miles we overtook some Yankee cavalry pickets, whom our sharpshooters, under Major Blackford, of the Fifth Alabama, quickly dispersed. We followed closely, and they evacuated Jeffersonton, falling back to the river, and crossing a bridge near Warrenton Springs. General Pendleton, chief of artillery, placed twelve pieces of cannon on a lofty hill immediately in front of my regiment and commenced a rapid and destructive fire across the river, driving the enemy some distance beyond. As soon as it was ascertained that they had left the banks of the Rappahannock, General Rodes ordered Battle's Alabama and Doles' Georgia brigades to push rapidly across, and it was promptly done amid a sharp fire from musketry and cannon. Battle's brigade was moved down the Warrenton turnpike by the old burnt hotel. Right here gallant J. E. B. Stuart galloped by with the Twelfth Virginia cavalry and charged right royally upon the Yanks, strongly posted on a hill in front, but the Virginians were too few in number and were forced to retire. General Battle was ordered to send a regiment to dislodge the enemy, and he selected the Twelfth Alabama for the honorable though dangerous task. The other regiments supported us some distance in the rear. We moved under a heavy fire to and through the woods towards the hills occupied by the enemy. When within forty yards the regiment fired a volley into them which seriously disconcerted them, and followed it by volley after volley until the enemy turned and fled. We followed with loud, rejoicing veils for some distance, until General Stuart halted us. I picked up a splendid Sharp's rifle in the commencement of the fight, procured some cartridges and fired three well aimed shots at the cavalrymen as they halted and fired at us. Some saddles were emptied. The Twelfth Alabama lost only two men killed and several wounded. The enemy, being on horseback, fired too high and overshot us. We killed and wounded many of them and captured a goodly number, with their fine horses and equipment. General Stuart highly complimented the conduct of the regiment, saying it was a very creditable and successful affair, of which the regiment and country had cause to feel proud. We slept on the battlefield, and were so tired as to need no better beds than the bare ground.

October 13. Marched to Warrenton by 12 o'clock. Sergeant Clower and I dined at Mrs. Cox's, and her pretty daughter, Miss Nannie, gave us some late Northern papers. They interested and amused us. Their boastings and misstatements of war movements are absurd.

Rose early, and while in line at "order arms," General Battle delivered an inspiring speech to each regiment. No one commands a braver, more reliable brigade than he. They never falter.

Battle of Bristow Station.

After marching a mile we overtook heavy skirmishing sharpshooters, and were soon exposed to shot and shell. Were under fire all the morning and larger part of the afternoon, and were marching and counter marching through fields and woods, and across hills and valleys. Ever and anon a bullet would strike some one and the victim would be hurriedly carried to the rear. Several were wounded. Crossed Cedar Run and marched on towards Manassas. Slept peacefully on Virginia soil near Bristow Station at night. Dear old mother Virginia has often, so often, furnished us with restful beds on her generous, hospitable bosom!

Several hundred Yankee prisoners were under guard near us, and much trading in knives, canteens, tents, biscuits, tobacco, etc., was carried on. The prisoners were very filthy, inferior looking men, mostly Germans.

Battle's brigade, and indeed most of Ewell's corps, were busily engaged tearing up crossties and railroad iron, burning the former and crooking the latter, all during a very heavy rain. Although wet to the skin, no man uttered a word of complaint, but all worked and talked in excellent humor. The irrepressible spirit, the wit and jollity of a Southern soldier cannot be overcome by any discomfort, neither heat nor cold, bleak winds nor scorching sunshine, sickness nor sorrow. After finishing; our share of the work we dried our dripping, wet clothes, erected the Yankee tents, which we had captured, and slept soundly and comfortably on the bare, cold, wet ground until morning. We were two and a half miles from Catlett's Station, on A. & R. R. R.

Major Proskauer, of the Twelfth Alabama, with half of each company, six commissioned and several non-commissioned officers, was sent down the railroad towards Warrenton Junction to destroy more of the road. Late in the afternoon the rest of the regiment joined us.

At 4 o'clock resumed our march, the Twelfth Alabama in front of the brigade, and Company F in front of the regiment. Soon passed Bealton, which the enemy had destroyed by fire. What a cruel sight, chimneys standing as lone sentinels, and blackened ashes around them, indicating reckless wantonness and cowardly vengeance upon helpless women and children. Even war, savage war, should be conducted upon more humane principles. Sword and musket and cannon are more tolerable, more courageous. Fire is the weapon of cowards of the most cruel and most beastly nature and the stealthy instrument of the inhuman. The place had been a Yankee depot of supplies. Bivouacked near Rappahannock Station, cold and frosty, but slept soundly. The surrounding country is deserted by its former inhabitants. I saw a splendid mansion without an occupant and in very dilapidated condition. The Yankee generals had used many of these mansions for their headquarters without any thought of paying for them.

Bugle call at 3 o'clock A. M., October 19th, and in half an hour we started for the river. We were soon overtaken by a very heavy fall of rain, hail and sleet, accompanied by a fierce driving wind, which blew off hats and almost changed one's course in walking. We crossed the

Rappahannock on a pontoon bridge, and marched through mud and slush and rain towards Kelly's Ford, and halted in an old field.

The brigade was suddenly ordered to cross river and protect from cavalry raids our wagons, which were hauling railroad iron. Marched eight miles, rested until sundown, and returned to quarters after dark.

The 12th and 26th Alabama, on October 27th, went on picket duty to Kelly's Ford, the former relieving the 14th North Carolina. I walked several miles around Kellysville, once the scene of a severe cavalry engagement, on a tour of observation. The country around about resembled Fauquier county, being one vast field of destruction and devastation. Where once elegant, happy homes stood, bare chimneys rear their tall forms, sentries over this cruel waste, halls that once resounded to the merry laughter of happy children, now re-echo to the mournful whistling of the autumn winds. Everything we see is a memento of the relentless cruelty of our invaders.

Some North Carolina troops relieved us from picket duty and returned to the building of our winter quarters on the 30th. Our Christian Association met and resolved to forbid playing cards for pastime or amusement. New officers for next two months, President, Rev. H. D. Moore; V. P., Capt. J. J. Nicholson, of Company I; Secretary, Wat. P. Zachry of Company F.

November 1. Sunday. Chaplain Moore preached two able sermons. Subject of one at night was "Repentance," and he explained that conviction, contrition, or sorrow, confession and reformation constitute repentance.

November 2. Major H. A. Whiting, of General Rodes' staff, and Lieutenant Dan Partridge, of General Battle's, inspected our brigade. I drew five splendid English overcoats and three blankets for Company F. How can I fairly issue or divide so few articles, so much needed this cold weather? These uncomplaining men are patriotic indeed. Sutler Sam Brewer arrived with a load of goods which he speedily sold out to clamoring, eager purchasers. He demands and gets $1.00 a pound for salt, $2.00 per dozen for common sized apples, $5.00 per pound for soda, $1.00 per quart for ground peas or "goobers," $3.00 a pound for lard, $6.00 a quart for syrup made of Chinese sugar cane, $1.00 for three porous ginger cakes, $1.00 per dozen for small, tough sugar cakes, $1.00 for a pound bale of Confederate coffee, made of rye. Those who use tobacco pay $4.00 a pound for it. This depreciation in our currency is trying to men who get $11.00 per month only. One dollar formerly bought more than eleven will now

Several of my company assisted me in building to the end of my tent a chimney of small, unskinned pine poles, which they covered pretty well with mud. Then they floored my tent, and I am comfortable and proud of my quarters. Very few of the men can procure plank for flooring, and their tents are surrounded by ditches to keep out rain and snow, and straw and hay are substituted for plank.

November 6. Suffered from neuralgia in my face, which has swollen considerable. Late in the day a terrible cannonading towards Kelly's Ford and Rappahannock Station surprised us, and our brigade, under Colonel O'Neal, of the Twenty-sixth Alabama, was marched rapidly to the Ford. Though in great pain, I commanded my company, and we were soon in line of battle and under a heavy shelling. This we had to endure for some time. Two North Carolina companies were captured by the Yankees in their rapid movement. At the station Hay's Louisiana, and Hoke's North Carolina brigades lost heavily in prisoners. The attack seems to have completely surprised our generals. Were in line of battle until 12 o'clock at night, then marched by the right flank across Mountain Run at Stone's Mill. Passed through Stephensburg, and went within two miles of Culpepper C. H. There halted and formed line of battle, Battle's brigade extending from top of a lofty hill, towards Brandy Station, and joined by Early's division. We began to throw up breastworks as a protection against shells in case of attack, in two different places, using our tin cups, plates and bayonets in place of spades and picks, of which we had none. How many earthworks have been quickly built in old Virginia by these simple implements! Orders came to stop our work and move to Raccoon Ford, which we reached at 9 o'clock at night, and crossed in great darkness. Colonel Pickens kindly gave me a seat on his horse behind him to cross Mountain Run and Rapidan river, and I was enabled to keep dry. After Rode's division waded the river, we were marched down to Morton's Ford, arriving at half past ten o'clock and halting at the old camp ground we occupied before our tramp to Bristow Station, after General Meade in October. Just one month from the time we left we returned. As sleep had been a stranger to me for two nights, I enjoyed it, and all neuralgic pains left me, and never returned.

Nov 9th to 18th. On picket duty and annoyed by constant alarms. On last day were suddenly aroused by rapid succession of shells in our midst, warning us of the dangerous proximity of our foes. The 6th Alabama had three men wounded on outpost. The 12th Alabama relieved them. Completed our rude fortifications and are ready to welcome Meade and his cohorts to hospitable graves.

Nov. 24th. Expected President Davis to review the corps today but the rain prevented. Our great leader must be sorely tried these gloomy days, and is evidently the "right man in the right place."

At 1 o'clock A. M., Nov 26th, we were suddenly aroused and hurried towards Jacob's Ford where Meade had crossed part of his army.

Battle of Locust Grove, Nov. 27th.

In afternoon near Locust Grove, we met the advance of the enemy, and our sharpshooters engaged them in a fierce skirmish until dark. While skirmishing, the brigade in the rear was busily employed throwing up breastworks of poles and earth, latter dug up with picks made of sharpened oak poles and bayonets, and thrown on the logs and brush with tin plates and cups and bare hands. It is marvelous with what rapidity a fortification sufficiently strong to resist minie balls can be thrown up. A sense of danger quickens a man's energies.

Battle of Mine Run, Nov 28th.

Before daylight our army fell back about two miles and we began constructing breastworks on a high hill west of Mine Run. The enemy soon appeared on the east side of Mine Run, and commenced exchanging shots with our sharpshooters. A heavy rain fell and added to our discomfort. By night Battle's brigade had thrown up works almost strong enough to resist bomb shells and cannon balls. Early on the 29th, the Yankees began a rapid and continuous shelling from their batteries, which caused us to seek protection behind our works. The wind blew fiercely and chilled us to the bone. In the afternoon we saw an adventurous Yankee regiment approach in line of battle, when Carter's battery opened on them, and the line broke and scattered in confusion. We could see several wounded men carried off on litters. We stayed in the trenches all night ready for a charge, a detail from each company remaining awake. The fierce, cold winds made sleep light and uncomfortable.

December 1, 1863. A remarkably quiet day Not a cannon shot fired and scarcely a report from a musket. Meade was plainly making some movement but we could not discover what. The intensely cold weather continues. I was told by some Yankee prisoners that some of their pickets were actually frozen to death while on post, and that others were carried off wholly insensible from cold. I can believe the story, as I never suffered more in my life.

December 2. We learned that Meade had crossed most of his force at Jacob's and Germanna Fords, and that the chance for a battle was now slight. We took the Germanna Ford road and hurriedly pursued, overtaking and capturing over 150 prisoners. Early and Johnson captured many on their respective roads. At night we went in direction of Morton's Ford, and slept in the woods.

The Confederate Congress is in session, and the papers publish President Davis' message, which I read with great interest and approval. His views about substitutes are excellent. My daily newspaper bills are heavy, as I take the *Richmond Dispatch* and the *Examiner*, and sometimes buy the *Whig* as well as the *Illustrated News*, price 50 cents each.

Sutler Brewer brought in some oysters and sold them at $20 a gallon. Messes club together and buy. I could not be a sutler. Their prices seem cruel and extortionate.

December 15. Sent private Tom Kimbrough to Orange Courthouse after boxes and trunk. Lieutenant George Wright came today. The trunk was mine and contained a large ham, pickles, a bushel or more of crackers, biscuit and cakes, a pair of boots and pair of pants. These came from home from the best of mothers, and anticipated Xmas. Lieutenant W brought a negro cook.

Our officers sent a memorial to the Secretary of War to transfer the Twelfth Alabama to Alabama for recruiting purposes, as we are opposed to consolidating with another regiment on account of our diminished ranks, until we have had a fair opportunity to recruit. The following is a copy of the petition:

"We, the undersigned officers of the Twelfth Alabama regiment, in behalf of ourselves and the men under our command, having the interest and good of the service at heart, in view of the recommendation of the Secretary of War, in his recent report to Congress, to consolidate the regiments which have fallen below the minimum required by law to retain their present organization, beg leave most respectfully to represent:

"That the Twelfth Alabama regiment has been in service in the field since July, 1861; and that in consequence of the ravages of disease and the casualties of battle in the hard fought fields of Virginia, Maryland and Pennsylvania, in which Rodes' old brigade has participated and acquired glory, the regiment has become reduced below the minimum; that the regiment is one of only two Alabama regiments which, within our knowledge, have not received any conscripts — and it being our desire to preserve intact the organization under which we have fought for now nearly three years — and to which we are attached by many hallowed memories of the past, by many associations of danger, trial, fatigue, hardship and suffering, and desiring that the name **"Twelfth Alabama"** be not obliterated from the rolls of the army.

"We, feeling perfectly convinced of our ability to recruit our shattered ranks by such a course, beg most respectfully that the regiment be transferred to Mobile, Ala., or some other point in the State, during the winter months, or until the opening of the spring campaign, then to return with full ranks to take our places once again with our comrades of the Army of Northern Virginia."

This petition is to be forwarded through the regular channels to General S. Cooper, Adjutant and Inspector General, C. S. A.

December 24. Christmas eve in the army bears no resemblance to the preparations at home for Christmas festivities.

Christmas Day. Ate a hearty dinner, minus the home turkey and cranberries and oysters and eggnog and fruit cake, and then wrote to my mother and sisters.

At 9 o'clock **Dec. 26,** Major Proskauer led the regiment towards Paine's Mills, where we were to relieve the 14th North Carolina, on fatigue duty, sawing plank for the Orange road, We lost the way and marched 20 miles to reach a mill only 12 miles distant from camp, arriving after dark. Companies F, B and C moved three miles from nearest mill to "Squire" Collins. Supped and breakfasted at the "Squire's." The 14th North Carolina desired to stay, and our regiment wished to return, so the engineer got an order from Gen. Lee permanently detailing the 14th North Carolina for this work.

General Lee issued an order directing that furloughs be furnished hereafter at the rate of four to the 100 men present for duty. I had a "drawing" in company F, and Win. Mimms drew the furlough and application was made for him. I addressed a letter of inquiry to Gen. R. H. Chilton, Chief of Staff, as to whether in the event an enlisted man obtained a recruit for his company, and actually enlisted him in service, the commanding General would grant the man so doing a furlough of 30 days?

Dec. 31, 1863. The last day of a most eventful year. It goes out in gloom; wet, muddy and still raining.

Jan. 1, 1864. New Year's Day. A very beautiful day. May the future of the South be as bright and glorious!

It is extremely cold, below zero. Major Whiting, Division Inspector, examined the arms and clothing of the men, and found them sadly in need of shoes, many of them being barefooted, and the others having no soles to their shoes, the uppers only remaining.

Sunday. Jan. 3rd. Summoned to brigade headquarters with Capt. R. M. Greene, of Opelika, from the 6th Alabama, and Lieut. Dunlap, of Mobile, from the 3rd Alabama, to investigate the stealing of two cows from the Misses Lee. We could obtain no light on the subject. Rations of all kinds are very scarce now. Only half a pound of bacon per day to each man, and this irregularly From three-quarters of a pound to a pound of flour and no vegetables, nor syrup, nor coffee, nor indeed ought else, per man. The hearty fellows get hungry.

Colonel Chilton, chief of General Lee's staff, on the 4th, answered my letter of inquiry of the 29th ult., and sent me a copy of "General Orders No. 1, Current Series, A. N. Va.," which granted furloughs to all enlisted men who actually mustered in a recruit in the Army of Northern Virginia. Wesley Moore telegraphed his brother, Micajah, who had just reached 18 years, to come on. I think the order will do great good, and I am gratified at having had such notice and approval taken of my suggestion. I wonder if my letter induced this famous "general order?"

A great snow fell during the night of January 8th. The water particles congealed into white crystals in the air, and sprinkled the ground about four inches deep. The regiment was ordered out to witness the execution of two deserters.

Battle's brigade left early for picket duty on the Rapidan river. I was left in camp as its commander, and have more men in camp, left on account of bare feet and bad shoes, than Colonel Goodgame carried oft with him.

I issued strict orders for the sentinels to walk their posts constantly, and to pass no man with a gun, and to arrest all who attempted to leave or enter camp with guns, without my written permission. I issued these orders because some of the men have already left with guns in search, I suspect, of hogs, cows or other things, belonging to citizens, that might be eaten. At night Lieutenant Karcher arrested eight men with guns and confined them in the guardhouse. As punishment I directed the prisoners to lay a causeway around the guard lines for the sentinels use.

January 17. Marched Company F to Captain Pickens' headquarters and they were paid for November and December, and commutation for clothing from December 12, 1862, to December 12, 1863. The men felt rich with their depreciated money. How cheerful and jocular they are!

January 21. Orders from General Lee to send applications for furloughs at rate of 12 to 100 men present. Tom Clower and Pierce Ware are the lucky ones.

January 26. This has been a bright, pleasant day, a most memorable one in the history of Battle's brigade. General Battle made speeches to each one of his regiments, and they re-enlisted unconditionally for the war. I never witnessed such unanimity upon a matter of such vital importance. The brave Twelfth Alabama, when the invitation was given to those who desired to volunteer to step forward two paces, moved forward as one man. General Battle spoke eloquently. Other officers spoke well. Battle's brigade is the first in the Army of Northern Virginia to re-enlist unconditionally for the war. This is an act of which we should well be proud to our dying day

January 27. General Battle sent the following communication to each regiment in his brigade:

"Headquarters Battle's Brigade, January 26, 1864.
The Brigade Commander has the pleasure of presenting the subjoined communication from Major-General Rodes:

"Headquarters Rodes' Division, January 26, 1864.
"Brigadier-General Battle, Commanding Battle's Brigade:
General, — I have just received your message by Captain J. P. Smith, informing me of the glorious conduct of my old brigade in re-enlisting for the war without conditions. Conduct like this, in the midst of the hardships we are enduring, and on the part of men who have fought so many bloody battles, is in the highest degree creditable to the men and officers of your command. I always was proud, and now still more so, that I once belonged to your brigade. As their division commander, and as a citizen of Alabama, I wish to express my joy and pride, and as a citizen of the Confederacy, my gratitude at their conduct. The significance of this grand movement, when considered in connection with the circumstances accompanying it, will not be underrated, either by the enemy or our own people. They will,

as I do, see in this the beginning of the end, the first dawn of peace and independence, because they will see that these men are unconquerable. To have been the leaders of this movement in this glorious army throws a halo of glory around your brigade which your associates in arms will recognize to envy, and which time will not dim. Convey this evidence, feebly at best, but doubly so in comparison with what I would express of my appreciation of the course you and your men have pursued in this matter, and see now, having written "Excelsior" in the records of your camp history, that your fighting record shall hereafter show you, not only to have been among the brave, but the bravest of the brave.

And now, dear sir, let me congratulate you upon being the commander of so noble a body of gallant and patriotic men!
(Signed) R. E. Rodes, Major-General."

June 6, 1864. About 8 o'clock Rodes' division packed up their baggage and marched down the breastworks near Richmond, and turning to the left at the same point as we did on the 30th of May, and continuing our course nearly a mile under a hot, broiling sun, when, coming up with Early's division, under Ramseur, and Gordon's division, we halted a few hours. At 2 o'clock P. M. we resumed our march towards the right flank of the enemy, going one mile, and then halting until dark. Skirmishing was brisk, and cannonading rapid in our front. We expected to be engaged at any moment, but something prevented, and we returned to a pine woods on the Mechanicsville turnpike, and remained during the night A good many straggling Yankees were captured, and reported the enemy moving to their left flank, and say their men are destitute of shoes, deficient in rations, and very tired of fighting, etc. They also report Burnside's negroes at the front. The enemy, unwilling to expose their own persons, not only invoke the aid of Ireland, Germany and the rest of Europe, but force our poor, deluded, ignorant slaves into their ranks. They will prove nothing but food for our bullets.

We remained in camp until evening, when we removed to a more pleasant locality. The enemy has disappeared from our left and left center, and gone towards our right, and Early's command enjoys a respite from the heavy and exhaustive duties of the past month.

Sergeant Gus P. Reid of my company, was appointed acting second lieutenant by Colonel Pickens, and assigned to command of Company D. The day was again marked by unusual quiet; cannon and musketry were seldom heard. I seized a moment to write a letter expressing sympathy to Mrs. Hendree, of Tuskegee, at the untimely death of her excellent and gallant son, Edward, who was killed May 5th at the Wilderness while commanding sharpshooters. The first twelve months of the war we were mess-mates and intimate friends. He was afterwards made first lieutenant in the Sixty-first Alabama. He was the only son of a widowed mother, and of exceeding great promise.

Remained in our bivouac until near 6 o'clock, when we were ordered to "pack up" and "fall in." Rev. Dr. William Brown preached to us. After his sermon we marched two miles towards the right of our line, and halted in an old field near an old Yankee camp, occupied by some of McClellan's troops before his memorable "change of base" in 1862. There we slept till near 3 o'clock next morning, when we were hurriedly aroused, but as we soon found out, needlessly.

There are rumors that Grant is mining towards our fortifications, and attempting his old Vicksburg maneuvers. But he will find he has Lee and Beauregard to deal with now. Mortars are said to be mounted, and actively used by both sides, on the right of our line. Appearances go to show Grant's inclination to besiege rather than charge Gen. Lee in the future. The fearful butchery of his drunken soldiers — his European hirelings — at Spotsylvania C. H., it seems, has taught him some caution. His recklessness in sacrificing his hired soldiery is heartless and cruel in the extreme. He looks upon his soldiers as mere machines, not human beings, and treats them accordingly.

Three years ago to-day, June 12, 1861, my company — "The Macon (County, Ala.) Confederates" — were enlisted as soldiers in the Provisional Army of the Confederate States, and I became a "sworn in" volunteer. I remember well the day the company took the prescribed oath to serve faithfully in the armies ‹of the Confederate States, and I can truthfully say I have labored to do my whole duty to the cause since then. Then I was a young Georgia student in an Alabama college, scarce 17 years of age, very unsophisticated in the ways of the world, totally unacquainted with military duties, war's rude alarms, and ever-present perils. Now I am something of a veteran, having served nearly one year as a private and two as a lieutenant, and being the larger part of the time in command of my company, composed principally of men much older than myself. I have participated in a great number of hotly contested battles and sharp skirmishes, have marched through hail and snow, rain and sleet, beneath hot, burning suns, and during bitter cold by day and by night, have bivouacked on bloody battle fields with arms in my hands, ready for the long roll's quick, alarming beat, have seen many a loved comrade, whose noble heart beat high with hope and bounded with patriotic love for his dear native South, slain by the cruel invader, and lying still in death's icy embrace. But despite the innumerable dangers I have passed through, through God's mercy, I am still alive, and able and willing to confront the enemies of my country.

At 2 o'clock in the morning of June 13th, my corps took up the line of march, some said to assume its position on the right of the army, and others to the south side of the James, still others thought it was a grand flank movement in which Grant was to be outgeneraled as McClellan was, and Lee, as usual, grandly triumphant. None of the numerous suppositions proved correct. Battle's Alabama brigade, under Colonel Pickens of the Twelfth Alabama, led the corps, and we crossed the Chickahominy and entered the Brook turnpike, five miles from Richmond. Here we turned towards Louisa Courthouse and halted near Trevillian's depot, seven miles from Gordonsville. On our route we passed the late cavalry battlefields, where Generals Hampton, Butler and Fitzhugh Lee defeated General Sheridan, *et als*. A great many dead and swollen horses on the ground, and graves of slain soldiers were quite numerous. The fight was too warmly contested.

Early's corps is now hotly pressing Hunter towards Liberty and Salem, Va. Yankee armies are seldom caught when they start on a retreat. In that branch of tactics they excel. They will run pell-mell, if they think it necessary Prudence with them is the better part of valor, and they bear in mind the lines from Butler's Hudibras —

> *"He who fights and runs away*
> *Will live to fight another day;*
> *But he who fights and is slain*
> *Will never live to fight again."*

June 23. I became quite ill, and was sent to hospital. But left Lynchburg hospital June 28th, joined my regiment two miles from Staunton, found the command ready for rapid marching, and packed my valise, retaining only an extra suit of underclothing. In my valise I left my diary, kept for two years past, and giving daily, brief accounts of all that has happened to myself and my immediate command. It is too large and heavy to carry along with me, though I have become very much attached to it — from such constant use and association — but I must make a virtue of necessity and entrust it to the keeping of an unknown and perhaps careless quartermaster. No officer's baggage wagons are allowed on the expedition, and all of us have left the greater portion of our clothing and all our company documents, papers, etc. In the afternoon we passed through Staunton and bivouacked six miles beyond, on the famous Valley turnpike.

We marched some distance on the turnpike, then turned to the right and halted near a little village called Keezeltown. Received notice from hospital of death of private Robert Wynn, of Auburn. Poor Bob! He had been married but a short time to the young sister of Sergeant R. F. Hall, and, soon after he joined us, he had an attack of pneumonia, which, together with nostalgia (a species of melancholy, common among our soldiers, arising from absence from home and loved ones), soon brought his young career to an end. Our valley army under that old bachelor, lawyer and soldier, Lieutenant-General Early, is composed of the small divisions of Major- Generals Robert E. Rodes, of Alabama, J. C. Breckinridge, of Kentucky, late vice-president of the United States, J. B. Gordon, of Georgia, and S. D. Ramseur, of North Carolina. All of them small — some of the brigades no larger than a full regiment, some of the regiments no larger than a good company, and many of the companies without a commissioned officer present, and having only a corporal's guard in number of enlisted men. We are all under the impression that we are going to invade Pennsylvania or Maryland. It will be a very daring movement, but all are ready and anxious for it. My own idea has long been that we should transfer the battle-ground to the enemy's territory, and let them feel some of the dire calamities of war.

Returned to the turnpike on 30th and marched eighteen miles, half mile beyond New Market. This place was the scene of the Dutch General Siegel's signal defeat by General Breckinridge. The men who "fit mit Siegel's" preferred running to fighting on that occasion.

July 1st, 1864. Marched 22 miles today, from New Market to two miles beyond Woodstock, where we remained for the night. This is the anniversary of the first day's battle at Gettysburg, and one year ago late in the afternoon, just before my brigade entered the city, I was wounded. I well remember the severe wound in the head received that day by Lieutenant Wright, near my side, and his earnest appeal to me to tell him candidly the nature of his terrible wound. I shall never forget the generous forgetfulness of self and warm friendship for myself shown by Captain Nicholson, of Company I, when the command was forced back by overwhelming numbers. I had been wounded, and fearing that I would be captured, hobbled off alter my regiment, as it fell back under a very close and galling fire from the rapidly advancing Yankees. Nicholson, noticing my painful efforts to escape, suddenly stopped, ran to me and catching my arm offered to aid me, but appreciating his well-meant kindness, I declined his proffered assistance and begged him to hurry on, telling him, to induce him to leave me and save himself, that I would stop unless he went on.

On July 3rd we marched through the historic old town of Winchester and encamped at Smithfield. The good people of Winchester received us very enthusiastically.

July 4. Declaration of Independence day, but, as we had other business before us, we did not celebrate the day in the old time style. We marched through Halltown to Charlestown near the old field where that fanatical murderer and abolitionist, John Brown, was hung, and halted under a heavy cannonading at Bolivar Heights, near Harper's Ferry. This place on the Baltimore and Ohio Railroad and the Potomac river, surrounded by elevated mountains, was once a United States arsenal and government foundry The Yankee camps had been hastily forsaken and our men quickly took possession of them and their contents. After dark General Battle took his brigade into the town where a universal pillaging of United States government property was carried on all night. The town was pretty thoroughly relieved of its stores, and the 4th of July was passed very pleasantly Corporal Henderson, while in a cherry tree, gathering fruit, was wounded by a minie ball and carried to hospital in the afternoon. Fuller H. is the son of Rev. S. Henderson, D. D., a noted Baptist minister of Alabama, and is a true and unflinching soldier. (Note. The poor fellow was editor, after the war, of the *Tuskegee News*, and for a few weeks, at his request, I edited the paper for him, as he was the owner, publisher, printer, editor and job printer, and overcrowded with his duties. During the time I wrote some mysterious orders, as if emanating from a Kuklux organization, signing them by order of "Grand Cyclops," calling upon the Klan to meet at a certain cave in the woods, near the town of Tuskegee, for the transaction of important business. Fuller, the night of the publication of the *News*, got out some posters and pasted them on the doors of certain stores in the town, and excitement and alarm was created by our innocent joke. There was no kuklux organization in or near Tuskegee, and it was our boyish prank. The result was that more than one carpetbagger left Alabama for his late home in the North.

In Company with Capt. James P. Smith, A. I. G,, and late of Stonewall Jackson's staff, Capt. Greene of the 6th Ala., and Sergt. Reid of my company. I returned to town in the morning and procured some envelopes, writing paper, preserved fruits, etc. The enemy's sharpshooters from Maryland Heights fired pretty close to us repeatedly, and bullets fell so rapidly it was dangerous to walk over the town, but as we were on a frolic, resolved to see everything and dare everything, we heeded the danger very little. We returned to camp near Halltown.

July 6. Rodes' and Ramseur's divisions crossed the Potomac at Shepherdstown, and marched through the famous town of Sharpsburg. Signs of the bloody battle fought there in Sept. 1862, between Lee and McClellan, were everywhere visible. Great holes, made by cannon balls and shells, were to be seen in the houses and chimneys, and trees, fences and houses showed countless marks made by innumerable minie balls. I took a very refreshing bath in Antietam creek, upon whose banks we bivouacked. Memories of scores of army comrades and childhood's friends, slain on the banks of this stream, came before my mind and kept away sleep for a long while. The preservation of such an undesirable union of States is not worth the life of a single Southerner, lost on that memorable battlefield. Lieut. John Fletcher of my company, from Auburn, and Capt. Tucker of Co. D commanding the 12th Alabama, were killed at Sharpsburg.

Left the Antietam and marched through a mountainous country towards Harper's Ferry, where constant cannonading could be heard. Our brigade halted near Rohrersville, three miles from Crampton's Gap, and the 3rd, 5th, 6th, 12th and 61st Ala., of which the brigade was composed, were sent in different directions to guard roads. The 12th Alabama was on picket all night, leaving outpost for the brigade at 3 o'clock P. M.

Rodes' division was taken within a short distance of the Ferry, halted for an hour or two, and then marched across the mountain at Crampton's Gap, where Gen. Howell Cobb's brigade of Georgians fought in 1862, and where Lieut-Col. Jeff Lamar, of Tom Cobb's Legion, was killed.

On **July 9th** we marched through and beyond Frederick City, but neither saw nor heard anything of the mythical "Barbara Freitchie," concerning whom the gentle Quaker poet, Whittier, erred sadly as to facts in his poem. We found the enemy, under Gen. Lew. Wallace, posted on the Heights, near Monocacy river. Our sharpshooters engaged them, and private Smith of Co. D was killed. Gen. Gordon attacked the enemy with his division, and routed them completely, killing a large number. Col. John Hill Lamar, of the 60th Georgia who had but six months before married the charming Mrs. Carter of Orange, Va., was killed. He was a brother of the wife of Capt. A. O. Bacon of Macon, Ga. There is a report that Gen. Early levied a contribution on Frederick City, calling for $50 000.00 in money, 4,500 suits of clothes, 4,000 pairs of shoes, and a quantity of bacon and flour. Battle's brigade was in line of battle all the evening, and marched from point to point, but was not actively engaged, though exposed to the fire of cannon and minie balls. Two divisions of the 6th Army Corps and some "hundred days men" opposed our advance. The latter were very easily demoralized and ran away.

Marched nearly twenty-five miles today, the 10th, on the main road to Washington City, passing through Urbana, Hyattstown, and other small places. It was a severe march.

At Washington City.

We passed through Rockville, and marched, under a very hot sun, towards Washington. Halted two miles from the inner fortifications, where we were exposed to a close and rapid shelling all the afternoon. The men are full of surmises as to our next course of action, and all are eager to enter the city. We can plainly see the dome of the capitol and other prominent buildings, Arlington Heights (General Lee's old home), and four lofty redoubts well manned with huge, frowning cannon. Several hundred pound shells burst over us, but only one or two men in the entire division were hurt. All the houses in our vicinity were vacated by their inmates on our approach, and the skirmishers in front were soon in them. Many articles of male and female attire were strewn over the ground. This conduct was against orders, but a few men led by an Italian, known as "Tony," who was once an organ grinder in Mobile, and now belonging' to the Guards LaFayette Company of my regiment, exerted themselves to imitate the vandalism of Hunter and Milroy, and their thieving followers, while they occupied the fair valley of Virginia. Private property ought to be — and is generally — respected by Confederate soldiers, and any other course is unmanly and unsoldiery. Yankee soldiers are not expected to appreciate such gentility and self respect. United States Postmaster Blair's house and farm were less than 100 yards from my regiment. General Breckinridge is an old acquaintance of General Blair, and had placed a guard around it, and forbade any one to enter the house, or at all disturb the premises. This course was in great contrast to that pursued by General Hunter when he caused the destruction of the residence of his cousin, Hon. Andrew Hunter, near Halltown, Va. Breckinridge is the very soul of honor, as are all our leading Generals. The meanest private in our army would not sanction the conduct of Milroy and Hunter.

Some heavy skirmishing occurred on the 12th and one of my regiment was wounded. The sharpshooters and Fifth Alabama, which supported them, were hotly engaged. Some of the enemy, seen behind breastworks, were dressed in citizens clothes and a few had on linen coats. I suppose these were "home guards," composed of treasury, post office and other department clerks. I went to Roche's and other houses near the picket line, and was shown some very disreputable letters, received and written by young ladies which had been found in the houses, and which exhibited the decadence of moral sentiment in the masses of the North. It was a day of conjecture and considerable excitement, in our momentary expectation of being ordered "forward." But we were disappointed in our expectation and wishes, and, late at night, we evacuated our position and left Washington and its frightened inhabitants. The object of the daring expedition was no doubt accomplished, and Grant was forced to send large re-enforcements to the threatened and demoralized capital from his army, and thus largely diminish his force and lessen his ability to act upon the offensive. I believe we could have taken the city when we first reached it, but the delay brought heavy battalions from Grant, ten times our small number, who could have readily forced us to abandon it. About 12 o'clock at night we commenced falling back towards Rockville, and, I regret to say, our march was brilliantly illuminated by the burning of the magnificent Blair mansion. The destruction of the house was much deplored by our general officers and the more thoughtful subordinates, as it has been our policy not to interfere with private property. It was set on fire, either by some thoughtless and reckless sharpshooter in the rear guard, or by some careless soldier stationed about the house.

Marched in retreat the remainder of the night, passed through the friendly Southern town of Rockville and halted near Darnestown.

At dusk we commenced marching, via Poolsville, to White's Ferry on the Potomac. Did not march over five miles the entire night, though kept awake, and moving short distances at intervals of a few minutes. Re-crossed the Potomac on the 14th, wading it, and halted near the delightful little town of Leesburg. We have secured, it is said, over three thousand horses and more than twenty-five hundred head of beef cattle by this expedition, and this gain will greatly help the Confederate government. The Yankee cavalry made a dash upon our wagon train and captured a few wagons. General Cook's Georgia and Battle's Alabama brigades were double-quicked, or rather ran, about two miles after them, but of course could not succeed in overtaking them. The idea of Confederate infantry trying to catch Yankee cavalry, especially when the latter is scared beyond its wits, is not a new one at all, and though attempted often in the past, and doubtless to be repeated scores of times in the future, I venture to predict, will never be successful. Indeed it is a demonstrated fact that demoralized and retreating Yankee infantry cannot be overtaken by Confederate cavalry, *vide* battles of Bull Run, Manassas, first and second, etc. A frightened Yankee is unapproachable. We finally gave up the pursuit and marched through Snicker's Gap. The Twelfth Alabama picketed on the mountain top. Next day we left our picket post and waded across the Shenandoah. The water rose to our waists and was quite swift, and as the bed of the river was rocky and uneven we had a good deal of fun. Some practical jokes were indulged in, which all seemed to enjoy. Rodes' division was hurriedly ordered out to meet the enemy, who had crossed the Shenandoah under General Crook, and in an incredibly short time we were hotly engaged in battle. The fight lasted over two hours, and was quite warmly contested. The Yankee force was three times greater than ours. Private Eberhart of my company was instantly killed. We had driven the enemy to the bank and in the river, and, having halted on a little eminence were peppering them with bullets as they rushed into and attempted to cross the river. They replied as best they could, but under great disadvantage. A large number remained concealed near the river, at the foot of the hill, and did some execution, firing at our men, as they exposed themselves. They escaped undercover of darkness. When Eberhart was killed, private Tom Kimbrough called me earnestly to him, and, through a heavy shower of bullets, I went to him and inquired what he wanted. "Nothing," he replied, "just thought you would like to see Eberhart after he was dead." A rather poor reason, I thought, for causing a man to unnecessarily expose himself to death-dealing missiles, I took care of his pocket book, his wife's ambrotype and Bible, and will send them to her. Eberhart was a brave, uncomplaining, good soldier, sent to my company as a conscript. Private G. P Ware, was severely wounded in the leg. Lieutenant Majors, of Company E, and two others of the regiment, were killed, and ten or fifteen wounded. Lieutenant Majors and I were running near each other in quick pursuit of the enemy, when he exclaimed that he was shot, but continued to run for some distance and then fell. I stopped by his side and offered him some water from canteen, which he hastily drank, and then sank down and instantly expired. A minie ball had cut an artery in his leg, but such was his determined courage, and eagerness in following the fleeing foe, that he ran on, his life-blood all the time gushing from his wound, and stopped only when sheer exhaustion and faintness from such great and rapid loss of blood compelled him, and the grim monster death claimed him for his own.

Majors had been but recently promoted, and was an officer of decided promise. In this action Col. Pickens commanded our brigade, and Lieut-Colonel Goodgame the regiment. While the routed and demoralized Yankees were crossing the river, I ordered my company, and those adjoining it, to fire by rank and by command, as in ordinary manual drill, the only instance of such an event, to my knowledge, during the war. I gave the words of command, "front rank," "ready" "aim," "fire," "load;" "rear ranks," "ready." etc., by consent of Col. Goodgame, and I confess I took much pleasure in it. While we were engaged burying our dead comrades, under a large tree near where they fell, Gen. Early and staff rode by, and the old hero spoke to us gently, and kindly suggested that we "dig the graves deep enough." A brave North Carolinian had somehow and somewhere come in possession of a silk hat, and had made himself conspicuous by wearing it, despite the advice and warning of his companions, and indeed of the whole division, as the men used to frequently to tell him, as he passed by, "to come down out of that hat," "I see your feet hanging from that stove pipe," etc., all of which he heard with cheerful good humor, generally making some witty reply. In walking over the battlefield I was pained to see the well known tall hat, and upon nearing it, recognized the handsome, good natured face and manly form of the gallant wearer, lying cold in death. He had been shot in the head.

On July 24th we were suddenly summoned to leave our picket

post for Winchester, marching very rapidly, forming line of battle near Kernstown, and moving quickly after the enemy, through Winchester, and five miles beyond, being in less than half a mile of the routed and flying Yankees almost the whole time. They, in their flight and haste to escape, burned up thirty five or forty wagons and caissons, and abandoned a few cannon. The entire movement was a very successful one. We marched fully thirty miles during the day. But, as I have said before, it seems to be impossible to catch a running Yankee. They are as fleet as race horses.

Today, July 29, we marched to Williamsport, Md., where our cavalry crossed the Potomac and captured large quantities of commissary and quartermasters' stores.

General John C. Breckinridge

Re-enlistment for the War.

In January, 1864, while encamped near Orange C. H., the Richmond and other Southern papers were filled with the proceedings of Congress, and discussions in regard to the passage of the Conscript Act, and the officers and men of Battle's Alabama brigade made it a topic of frequent conversation. The preference of myself and many officers of companies, which had enlisted for two more years, that would expire during the spring and summer, was to volunteer for the remainder of the war, however long, and thus avoid the necessity, and what we thought was the stigma, that would attend conscription. Having this thought in view, with others, I was active in calling together delegates from the various companies in our brigade to a convention to be held at the quarters of the 12th Alabama.

The following day, promptly at eleven o'clock, every company in the brigade had a delegate present. Nearly all of these delegates were non-commissioned officers or privates, chosen by their respective companies, but my company selected me as its representative, and Lieut. P. H. Larey of Co. M 6th Alabama, was chosen by his company, and Capt. Thos. Bilbro of the 3rd Alabama by his. On assembling, some one nominated me for Chairman of the Convention, and I was chosen without opposition, with Sergt. Sprague of Co. C, 3rd Alabama, as Secretary.

The subjects of re-enlistment, and petition to Congress for the privilege of reorganization, and the election of our field and company officers, were earnestly and eloquently discussed and advocated by all of the delegates, so far as I recall, except Capt. W. T. Bilbro and Sergt. Sprague. Lieut. Larey made an able speech, advocating the privilege of reorganization, and petitioning Congress for this permission. After a frank debate, upon putting the vote, it was found to be unanimous, with but two exceptions, and our petition was duly drawn up, signed and forwarded to Hon. David Clopton, M. C. from Alabama, and Senator Jemison, with the earnest request that they advocate the granting of the petition by Congress.

A few days later, Gen. Battle visited each regiment and delivered an eloquent address, urging the men to volunteer for the war, which was gallantly responded to by the men stepping forward and expressing their determination to enlist. It was an inspiring sight to see these heroes step forward without hesitation and boldly announce their purpose to continue the fight to the bitter end. This was their third enlistment.

Gen. Rodes issued a complimentary address, which was read before each regiment, in which he expressed his gratification at the re-enlistment of his old brigade of Alabamians, and at their leading the entire army in this noble action.

Gen. Lee in a letter addressed to Hon. T J. Foster, dated Jan. 31, 1864, used these words:

"I do not see how the good of the service can be promoted by detaching the 26th Alabama, thus breaking up a veteran brigade which has just set the glorious example in this Army of re-enlistment for the war. « Further on he says: «General Rodes' whole division acted at Chancellorsville with distinguished gallantry, and that officer owes his promotion to General Jackson's observation of his skill and conduct, and you will see by my report of that battle that one of his dying messages to me was to the effect that General Rodes should be promoted Major General, and his promotion should date May 2nd. He commanded his division with success and ability, and I am gratified to state that his division has re-enlisted for the war, Battle's brigade of Alabamians having set the example. Instead of raising new brigades I think it would be far better to recruit to the fullest number those veteran brigades whose whole conduct is worthy of the admiration of the country."
Respectfully,
Your obedient servant, (Signed) R. E. Lee, General.

Congress did not act favorably upon our petition, but passed a sweeping and peremptory act conscripting everybody in the Confederacy, (above the age of sixteen and under that of forty-five), to active military service. This was quite a disappointment to many gallant officers who desired and deserved promotion after their three years of experience, and many brave and intelligent privates who were worthy to command companies and even regiments.

In my own company F, there were near a score of non-commissioned officers and privates promoted to commissioned officers, and there were many among them who were never promoted who were entirely worthy and well qualified to fill positions of trust and honor. There were nearly one dozen college boys in the company, several of my own classmates, and there were a large number of lawyers, merchants and farmers. The combined wealth of the one hundred and six volunteers, who left Tuskegee the last of May, 1861, for Richmond, was estimated at more than a million dollars. Such men as Hon. Bython B. Smith, a lawyer of wealth and intelligence, Hon. Nicholas Gachet, a distinguished lawyer of large means, James F. Park, of the Tuskegee Classical Institute, who, since the war, has been honored with the distinctions of Ph. D. and LL. D., now living at LaGrange, Ga., and lately mayor of that city, H. R. Thorpe, M. D., from Auburn, a prominent physician, who was promoted to assistant surgeon of a North Carolina regiment, and a very large number of younger men, belonging to the first families in Alabama, and the sons of parents of prominence, influence and wealth. Sergeant Jack Echols, afterwards Colonel C. S A., and whose father was also a colonel, Judge Clopton, Congressman, and Lieutenant Governor Ligon, were all owners of many slaves and much landed property.

August 3, 1864. At Bunker Hill for three days. This rest and quiet, after our continual marching and counter marching, double-quicking, running, fighting, skirmishing, long-roll alarms by day and by night, loss of sleep by night marches and constant picketing, is generally enjoyed by us all.

On August 4th we left our quiet camp for Maryland, and passed through Martinsburg, halting six miles beyond.

Waded across the Potomac at Williamsport, and marched towards Boonsboro, halting five miles from Funkstown. General Breckinridge's command crossed at Shepherdstown. The majority of the men took off their shoes, tied them on their knapsacks, and waded through, over the rocks and gravel, barefoot,

Breckinridge's corps, consisting of his own and Wharton's small divisions, passed by us and crossed the Potomac. General Breckinridge was formerly vice-president of the United States, and is a magnificent looking man, weighing over 200 pounds. He wears a heavy mustache but no beard, and his large piercing blue eyes are really superb. Rodes' and Ramseur's divisions also crossed to the Virginia side, wading the river again. We marched to the vicinity of Hedgesville and camped for the night.

This, August 14th, rude breastworks of rails were thrown up, but the enemy kept aloof Although we have thrown up scores of earthworks we have never been called upon to fight behind them.

August 17. We left our post for Winchester, and, on our route, saw where several large barns, loaded with wheat, corn and hay, had been burnt by order of General Sheridan. One large flouring mill of great necessity to the locality, had been destroyed. I suppose Sheridan proposes to starve out the citizens, or rather the women and children, of the valley (for the men are in the army), as well as Early's troops. Grant and he have resolved to make this fertile valley a desert, and, as they express it, cause it "to be so desolate that the birds of passage cannot find enough to subsist upon." This is a very ungenerous return for the humane manner in which General Lee conducted his Pennsylvania campaign last year, and for the very kind treatment of the citizens of Maryland and Pennsylvania by General Early and his command recently. Such warfare is a disgrace to civilization, but I suppose that Irish Yankee, Sheridan, and that drunken butcher and tanner, Grant, have little comprehension of sentiments of humanity or Christianity. Breckinridge and Gordon whipped the Yankees badly today in some severe skirmishing. Rodes, for a wonder, was not engaged. My good mother says Rodes' division is in every battle her papers mention, and that such expressions as "Rodes bore the brunt of the battle," "Rodes began the action," "Rodes' division led the advance" or "Rodes conducted the retreat, serving as rear guard," are constantly in the telegraphic columns, and to be found in "Letters from war correspondents." It is true that our gallant and beloved major general is usually foremost at the post of honor and danger. He is ably seconded by his efficient adjutants, Major H. A. Whiting and Major Green Peyton. Reinforcements from Longstreet's corps have reached us, and vigorous work may be expected. Lieutenant-General Anderson is in command.

We marched through Winchester, and were, as usual, warmly greeted. Ladies and children and negro servants stood on the porches and sidewalks, with prepared food of a very tempting kind, and goblets and pitchers of cool, fresh water, which they smilingly handed to the tired troops, who seldom declined the proffered kindness. The native Virginians of Winchester and the Valley are as true as steel, and the ladies — God bless and protect them! — are as heroic and self-denying as were the noble Spartan mothers. Indeed they are the equals of the highest, truest heroines of the grandest days of the greatest countries. The joy they evince, when we enter their city, serves to encourage and inspire us, and the sorrow we see in their fair countenances, and often hear them express, with trembling lips and streaming eyes, as we leave them to endure the cruel and cowardly insults and petty persecutions of Sheridan's hirelings fill our hearts with indescribable regret. We love to fight for patriotic Winchester and her peerless women. We camped one mile from Winchester on the Berryville Pike and cooked our rations. Lieutenant-General Anderson, with Kershaw's infantry and Fitz Lee's cavalry, arrived from Lee's army. Their ranks are much depleted, but a very small reinforcement will greatly encourage and help our sadly diminished command.

Today, August 19, we marched to our familiar old camping ground, the oft visited Bunker Hill.

On August 21 we marched through Smithfield, and halted about two miles from Charlestown, where "old John Brown's body" once "was mouldering in the ground, but is now marching on to h_ _ll." Our gallant division sharpshooters, under Colonel J. C. Brown, of North Carolina, those from our brigade, under Major Blackford, of the Fifth Alabama, and our regiment, under Lieutenant Jones, Company I, skirmished vigorously the rest of the day. The firing was fierce and continuous.

The Yankees fell back towards Harper's Ferry, and we promptly followed, passing their breastworks and through Charlestown, encamping in a woods near where Hon. Andrew Hunter's beautiful residence recently stood. His splendid mansion had been burnt by order of General (Yankee) Hunter, his cousin.

Here a sharp skirmish took place, in front of our camp, which we could see very plainly. It was a deeply interesting sight to watch them advancing and retreating, firing from behind trees and rocks and clumps of bushes, falling down to load their discharged muskets, and rising quickly, moving forward, aiming and firing again — the whole line occasionally running quickly forward, firing as they ran, with loud "rebel yells," and the Yankees retreating as rapidly, and firing as they fell back. It is so seldom we have an opportunity to look on, being generally interested combatants ourselves, that the exciting scene was very enjoyable. After dark the 12th Alabama relieved the brigade sharpshooters, and took the outer picket post.

August 25. At sun-up we were relieved in turn, and had to vacate the rifle pits under the fire of the enemy, General Anderson, with General Kershaw's division, took our place, and General Early, with the rest of the little army of the Valley, marched towards Shepherdstown on the Potomac. We met the enemy's cavalry beyond Leetown, but they fell back quickly, and except a few shells thrown at us, our advance was not opposed. We marched through Shepherdstown after dark, making the air ring with joyous shouts. Many ladies welcomed us with waving handkerchiefs and kind words, as we passed through the streets. Lieutenant Arrington, A. D. C. to General Rodes, was severely wounded in the knee, and Colonel Monaghan of Louisiana, commanding Hays' brigade, was killed in a skirmish today.

A convention of Yankee politicians is to be held at Chicago today, the 29th. I reckon they will spout a good deal about the "glorious Union," "the best government the world ever saw," the "stars and stripes," "rebels," "traitors," *et idonme*. Our entire corps was in line of battle all day, and General Breckinridge drove the enemy some distance from his front. The 12th Alabama went on picket at night.

August 31. Another reconnaissance by Rodes' Division. General Rodes received orders to drive the Yankees out of Martinsburg, and taking his division of Battle's Alabama, Cook's Georgia, Cox's North Carolina, and Lewis' North Carolina brigades, started on his errand. Battle's brigade was in front and was shelled severely. General Rodes seems to think his old brigade of Alabamians entitled to the post of honor, and usually sends them to the front in time of danger. About two miles out of town, the brigade was deployed and ordered forward. We marched in this way, through Cemetery Hill, into town, running out the Yankee cavalry and artillery under Averill.

At night we returned to our old camp, having made twenty-two miles during the day. These reconnaissances may be very important, and very interesting to general and field officers who ride, but those of the line and fighting privates wish they were less frequent, or less tiresome this sultry weather. We have walked this pike road so often that we know not only every house, fence, spring and shade tree, but very many of the citizens, their wives and children.

On **September 2nd** we marched toward Winchester, and when five miles distant met our cavalry, under General Yaughan, of Tennessee, retreating, the Yankees in pursuit. We quickly formed line, and moved forward, but the enemy retired, declining further battle. Camped six miles from Bunker Hill.

Today, **September 3rd**, we went to our well known resting point, Bunker Hill. A few shells were fired, and one wounded our skillful and popular surgeon, Dr. George Whitfield, from Demopolis, in the arm.

September 4th, Sunday. Marched towards Berryville, passing Jordan Springs, a well known watering place, and halted at 12 o'clock, one and a half miles from Berryville. Deployed to the left of the town, where we could see the enemy and their breastworks very plainly At night retired one mile.

September 5. Our division again passed Jordan Springs, and soon after hearing the skirmishers firing in front, were hastily formed into line, and ordered forward to support our cavalry, marching parallel with the pike. We pursued the enemy about four miles, during a heavy, drenching rain, amidst mud and slush, across cornfields, fences, ditches and creeks, but were unable to overtake them, and halted about three miles from Bunker Hill. It rained incessantly during the night, and prevented our sleeping very soundly. We hear very heavy skirmishing on the Millwood Road, and are ordered to be ready for action. Adjutant Gayle and Sergeant Major Bruce Davis keep busy carrying such orders from company o company. The Richmond papers bring us news of the fall of Atlanta. It grieves us much. Atlanta is between us and our homes. It is only seventy miles from where my dearly loved mother and sisters live, and all mail communication with them is now cut off. It pains and distresses me to think that La Grange and Greenville, Ga., may be visited by raiding parties, and my relatives and friends annoyed and insulted by the cruel Yankees, as the noble and unconquered people of the Valley have been.

Am daily expecting my commission as captain, as Capt. McNeely has been "retired" on account of the wound he received at Chancellorsville, May 3rd, 1863, nearly eighteen months ago, and since which time, except on wounded leave of absence, for twenty-five days, after the battle of Gettysburg, I have been in constant command of my company, being the only officer "present for duty." My commission will date from time of issuance of Captain McNeely's papers of retirement, some months since. Lieutenant Colonel Goodgame left for Alabama today on "leave of absence." His name is an exceedingly appropriate one, as he is a gallant, unflinching officer and soldier. His "game" is unquestionably "good." Company F was on picket today. 9th of September. I took tea with the family of Mr. Payne, near Stephenson's depot. They are true Southerners. Miss Betty Payne, the elder sister, is a very bright and accomplished woman. Our entire army is getting its supplies of flour by cutting and threshing the wheat in the fields, and then having it ground at the few mills the enemy have not yet destroyed. The work is done by details from different regiments. It shows to what straits we have been reduced. Still the men remain cheerful and hopeful.

September 10. Rodes' division, preceded by our cavalry, under Generals Fitz Lee and Rosser, went as far as Darkesville, returning to Bunker Hill at night. Our brigade acted as the immediate support of the cavalry. As it rained without cessation during the night, we had a very damp time of it. I slept on half, and covered with the other half, of my oil cloth, one I had obtained from the Yankees when I captured my sword. The drops of rain would fall from the leaves of the large trees under which I lay, drop on my head and face, and trickle down my back occasionally. Notwithstanding these little annoyances, I managed to get a pretty good night's rest. A stone served as my pillow.

I am almost barefoot, and was glad to pick up, and substitute for one of mine, an old shoe, which I found thrown away on the roadside. It, in its turn, may have been thrown away for a better one, or perhaps the wearer may, in some of the numerous skirmishes in this vicinity, have been wounded and lost his leg, thus rendering his shoe no longer necessary to him, or, probably, the gallant wearer may have been slain, and is now sleeping his last sleep in an unmarked and unknown soldier's grave. Nearly all of my company are barefoot, and most of them are almost destitute of pants. Such constant marching on rough, rocky roads, and sleeping on the bare ground, will naturally wear out the best of shoes and thickest of trousers. While anxious for some attention from our quartermasters, our men are nevertheless patient and uncomplaining. We returned at night to our camp near Stephenson's depot.

On **September 13th** in obedience to a singular order, we marched from our camp two or three miles in the direction of Winchester, and then marched back again. At night Company F went on picket This continual moving to and fro indicates that a decisive action is imminent. Sheridan is reported to have large reinforcements from Grant. Our own ranks are thinner than at any time since we entered service. My company is one of the largest in the 12th Alabama and numbers less than 30 "present for duty." The entire regiment, including officers, will not number 200, and the brigade is not more than 1,000 strong, if so much. It is said that Early has, including infantry, cavalry and artillery, less than 8,000 men for duty. General Anderson, with his infantry and artillery, has left us and returned to Richmond, leaving only Fitz Lee's small force of cavalry. On the other hand rumor says Sheridan has fully 40,000 well equipped, well clad and well fed soldiers. If Early had half as many he would soon have sole possession of the valley, and Sheridan would share the fate of Milroy, Banks, Shields, Fremont, McDowell, Hunter, and his other Yankee predecessors in the valley campaign. Sheridan's lack of vigor, or extra caution, very strongly resembles incompetency, or cowardice.

Anniversary of the Battle of Boonsboro, Maryland.

September 14. This is the second anniversary of the battle of Boonsboro, where I had the ill luck to be taken prisoner in 1862, and kept 90 days before being exchanged. We had just reached the scene of action, met the dead body of gallant Gen. Garland, when an order from General D. H. Hill, through General Rodes, to Colonel B. B. Gayle, of the 12th Alabama, directed that skirmishers should be deployed in front, and while our precise Adjutant, L. Gayle, was looking over his roster of officers, to detail one in his regular turn, Gayle hurriedly exclaimed, "detail Lieutenant Park to command the skirmishers," and I immediately reported for orders. Was directed to carry my squad of forty men, four from each company, to the foot of South Mountain, and "keep the enemy back." I hastily deployed the men, and we moved down the mountain side. On our way we could see the enemy in the valley below advancing, preceded by their dense line of skirmishers. I concealed my men behind trees, rocks and bushes, and cautioned them to aim well before firing. We awaited with bated breath and beating hearts, the sure and steady approach of the "Pennsylvania Bucktails," who were in front of us, and soon near enough to fire upon. In response to my loud command the men fired, almost simultaneously, and we drove back the skirmishers to their main line. The solid, well drilled line advanced steadily forward, and my small party, as soon as they were near enough to make their aim sure, fired again, and every leaden messenger sped on its unerring way and stilled a soldier's heart. At least fifty must have been killed or wounded by these two volleys. But they continued to advance, their officers cursing loudly, and earnestly exhorting them to "close up," and "forward." My men slowly fell back, firing from everything which served to screen them from observation. Several of them were wounded and six or eight became completely demoralized by the unbroken front of the rapidly approaching enemy, and despite my commands, entreaties and threats left me, and hastily fled to the rear. Brave Corporal Myers, of Mobile, adopting a suggestion of mine, aimed and fired at an exposed officer, receiving a mortal wound in the breast as he did so. I raised him tenderly, offered him water, and was rising to reluctantly abandon him to his fate, when a dozen muskets were pointed at me, and I was ordered to surrender. There was a ravine to our left, and the 3rd Alabama skirmishers having fallen back, the Yankees had got in my rear, and at the same time closed upon me in front. If I had not gone to Myers when he fell, I might have escaped capture, but I was mortified and humiliated by the necessity of yielding myself a prisoner. Certain death was the only alternative. One of the men, who ran away early in the action, reported that I had been killed, and my name was so published in the Richmond papers, and my relatives mourned me as one dead, until I was regularly exchanged and reached Richmond. The enemy pushed forward after my capture, and soon came upon Colonel Gayle and the rear support. He was ordered to surrender, but, drawing his pistol and firing in their faces, he exclaimed: "We are flanked, boys, but let's die in our tracks," and continued to fire until he was literally riddled by bullets, and surrendered up his pure, brave young spirit to the God who gave it. Colonel Gayle was originally from Portsmouth, Va. Lieutenant Colonel S. B. Pickens was severely wounded also, and the regiment fell to the command of Captain Exon Tucker, of Company D, who was killed at Sharpsburg three days afterwards.

Thoughts of that day's conflict bring to mind the names and faces of many of my noble company, very few of whom are still with me. I am grateful that such gallant spirits as Sergeants T. H. Clower, R. H. Stafford, A. P. Reid, J. H. Eason, W. M. Carr, and A. G. Howard, and privates P. W. Chappell, C. C. Davis, Pierce Ware, Tobe Ward, Lester, Moore, Attaway, and a few others are still spared as my faithful comrades and as true soldiers of the Confederacy. I am proud of them all, and regret that I can do so little for their comfort. All are worthy of commissions, and some would fill high positions most creditably.

Late in the afternoon of today we were relieved from picket and returned to camp, where I have written down these thoughts of the stirring incidents of this day two years ago. Captain Dan Partridge, of Selma, is now our excellent brigade ordnance officer, and is ably assisted by Sergeant A. G. Howard, a disabled soldier of my company.

Many "grapevine" telegraph reports are afloat in camp. None worthy of credence, but those of a cheerful nature exert a good influence over the tired soldier.

September 17. Rodes' and Gordon's divisions, with Braxton's artillery, marched to Bunker Hill.

Next day Gordon's division, with Lomax's cavalry, moved on to Martinsburg, and drove Averill's cavalry out of town, across the Opequon, and then returned to Bunker Hill. The Twelfth Alabama was on picket after dark. By referring to previous pages, I find we have camped at Bunker Hill July 25th and 31st, and August 1st, 2nd, 3rd,

7th, 8th, 9th, 19th, 20th, 27th, 28th, 29th and 30th, September 3rd, 10th and 17th. It seems to be a strategic point.

Grant is with the ruthless robber Sheridan today, and we expect an early advance. His force has been largely increased, while ours has been greatly diminished.

Battle of Winchester, September 19th, 1864.

Early this morning our cavalry pickets on the Opequon were driven in, and it became evident that an engagement was imminent. News came that the cavalry under Fitz Lee and Lomax, and Ramseur's division of less than 2,000 infantry, were engaged by the enemy near Winchester, and Rodes' division left Stephenson's depot to go to their assistance. Gordon's division preceded us, and as soon as we reached Ramseur, we were ordered to "forward into line," and almost as quick as thought, we were rapidly hurried to the attack. General C. A. Evans, Georgia brigade, meeting overwhelming columns of the enemy, was forced back through the woods, and the Yankees were pressing after them, and came near capturing some of our artillery, when Colonel Carter and Lieutenant Colonel Braxton opened on them with grape and canister, and the Yankees halted, and then fell back. As they began to fall back, Battle's brigade, which had formed in the rear of Evans, rushed forward and swept, with loud shouts, through the woods, driving the enemy swiftly before it. I commanded the right company of our regiment and brigade in the charge. Colonel Pickens was not far from me, and General Early himself rode near me as we entered the action. I lifted my hat to the old hero as we ran forward, and noticed how proudly he watched our impetuous advance. The enemy soon ran precipitately before us, and officers and men were in the utmost confusion. We raised the well known "rebel yell," and continued our onward run, for we actually ran, at our greatest speed, after the disordered host in our front. We could see that they had a much larger force than ours, but we cared not for numbers. We had never regarded superior numbers since we entered the service, in fact, we rather enjoyed it. The victory was then more creditable to us. We learned afterwards that the Sixth and Nineteenth army corps, with their full ranks and splendid equipment, were our opponents. As we moved forward we passed scores, yes, hundreds, of dead and wounded Yankees, and a large number of prisoners were captured. We passed entirely through the woods and into the open space beyond, when we halted for a moment, and then formed our line in the edge of the woods. While the lines were being established, Major Peyton, A. A. G. to General Rodes, rode up, and an indescribable, unexplainable something, I know not what, carried me to his side, as he sat motionless upon his horse. I had heard nothing, not even a rumor, nor whispered suggestion, yet something impelled me to ask, in a low tone, "Major, has General Rodes been killed?" In an equally low, subdued tone that gallant officer answered, "yes, but keep it to yourself, do not let your men know it." "Then who succeeds to the command of this division?" I asked. "General Battle," said he, and rode on to the next brigade. The dreadful news of Major General Rodes' sudden death, at such a critical moment, distressed and grieved me beyond expression. There was no better officer in the entire army than he, very few as brave, skillful and thoroughly trained. His men regarded him as second only to General Lee, excelled by none other. Robert E. Rodes was born at Lynchburg, Va., and graduated at the Virginia Military Institute, served two years as assistant professor, and afterwards became chief engineer of the A. & C. R. R. of Alabama. He entered the army as captain of a company from Tuscaloosa, was elected Colonel of the Fifth Alabama, and soon after promoted to brigadier-general, and succeeded General Ewell in command of the Fifth, Sixth and Twelfth Alabama and Twelfth Mississippi. The latter regiment was transferred, and its place supplied by the Third and Twenty-sixth Alabama. He was wounded at Seven Pines and Sharpsburg At Chancellorsville, in command of D. H. Hill's old division, he led the advance and swept everything before him. His clarion voice shouting, "forward men, over friend or foe," electrified his troops, and they were irresistible. They pushed on, under his gallant leadership, and completely routed the panic-stricken soldiers of "Fighting Joe" Hooker. After Generals Jackson and A. P Hill were wounded, General Rodes was in supreme command, but he modestly and patriotically yielded to General J. E. B. Stuart, who had been sent for by General Pendleton of the artillery. After this battle he was promoted to full major general, and put in charge of Battle's, Ramseur's (now Cox's), Doles' (now Cook's), and Daniel's (now Lewis') brigades. General Rodes was a precise and somewhat stern military man, of resolute expression and soldiery bearing, and enjoyed the implicit confidence of his superior officers as well as his troops. A fragment of shell struck him behind the ear, and in a few hours this brave, skillful and trusted officer yielded up his heroic life as a holocaust to his country's cause. He married the accomplished Miss Virginia Hortense Woodruff, of Tuscaloosa, Ala., who survives with a son, his namesake, and a younger daughter, Bell Yancey. The young and gallant Colonel S. B. Pickens, of the Twelfth Alabama, took command of the brigade as senior colonel. He has commanded it nearly the entire time since we left Richmond. He was wounded during the engagement. The enemy had Crook's full, fresh corps and all his heavy force of cavalry as a reserve, and they came to the rescue of the defeated and routed Sixth and Nineteenth corps. Our ranks were very thin indeed, and our lines stretched out far too much. The enemy overlapped us for hundreds, I might say, thousands of yards, and we had no fresh troops in our rear to come to our aid. Sheridan must have had six to our one, yet our weakened forces held their ground, obstinately and proudly, until late in the afternoon, when Crook's fresh division drove back our small cavalry force under Fitz Lee. General Breckinridge, with Wharton's attenuated division, repulsed them, but the troops soon became impressed with the horrible, unendurable idea that they were flanked, and began to retreat in confusion. Just before this idea became prevalent, private John Attaway, of my company, was shot through the breast by a minie ball, and called me, as he fell, to go to him, saying he was mortally wounded. I immediately began to walk from the right towards the left of the company where Attaway was lying, bleeding and faint. I had gone but a few steps, and, while raising my right foot, was struck in the calf of the left leg: by a minie ball, which broke the small (fibula) bone and badly fractured the large one. The ball flattened and came out sideways, severing muscles, veins, tendons and nerves. I was knocked down, but ordered two of my men to carry Attaway off the field, the brave and faithful fellow urging them to carry me off first, declaring he would die any way, and that my life must be saved. However, I had him moved away to the rear, before I consented for privates P. W. Chappell and Tobe Ward to place me on a blanket, and carry me to the rear. As I was borne back, Attaway called out for them to hasten with me out of danger, as bullets and shells and solid shot were flying thick and fast around us. His conduct was that of a true, magnanimous friend and generous soldier. Ward and Chappell carried me as gently and quickly as possible toward some ambulances in the rear When we reached them we were told they belonged to the Louisiana brigade, and I was refused admittance into one. At this time the gigantic and gallant Colonel Peck, who had been wounded and retired from the field, rode up, and ascertaining the state of affairs, ordered the men to "take him up tenderly and put him in an ambulance," adding, "he is a wounded brother soldier and must be cared for."

I thanked the Colonel, but he, in his bluff, soldierly way, interrupted and said he "had done nothing but what I would have done for him." Bidding a last farewell to my faithful men, I was driven to the Union Hotel, then turned into a hospital. (Note — Chappell and Ward were both afterward killed at Petersburg.) The surgeon examined my wound, and pronounced it a serious one, and dressed it, uncertain whether the leg should be amputated or not. In my own mind I resolved to die before submitting to its loss. The surgeon promised me, in event our army was to evacuate Winchester, to send me away in an ambulance, but a few minutes after shot and shell were fired into the Hospital building, crashing recklessly through roof, walls, chimneys, etc., and knocking down bricks, plastering, planks and splinters over the helpless wounded and dying, and the demoralized surgeons, hastily detailing two or three of their number to remain with the wounded, fled incontinently, forgetting, in their anxiety to escape capture, all thought of their promise to carry me along with them. Our scattered troops, closely followed by the large army of pursuers, retreated rapidly and in disorder through the city. It was a sad, humiliating sight, but such a handful of worn out men could not successfully withstand such overwhelming odds. I never saw our troops in such confusion before. It is said that Mrs. General Gordon, Mrs. Hugh Lee, and other patriotic ladies, ran impetuously into the streets and eloquently pleaded with the retreating soldiers to cease their flight and stand and confront the advancing enemy. Night found Sheridan's hosts in full and exultant possession of much abused Winchester. The hotel hospital was pretty full of desperately wounded and dying Confederates. The entire building was shrouded in darkness during the dreadful night. Sleep was impossible, as the groans, shrieks, sighs, prayers and oaths of the wretched sufferers, combined with my own severe pain, banished all thought of rest. Capt. Hewlett, of Co. H, wounded in the thigh, lay on the floor beside me. Wat Zachry, Sergeant Carr and Tom Crawford, wounded men of my company, made their escape from the city just as the Yankee cavalry entered in. A few noble women of Winchester ventured, with lanterns in their hands, to walk among the wounded and distribute sandwiches and cups of coffee with cheering words of comfort and sympathy One sweet, Christian woman came to me and stooping, placed her gentle hand on my pale forehead and said, "my poor boy, you seem to be in much pain, though so quiet, take some refreshments, and tomorrow you shall have a better bed than this hard floor." I thanked her, drank some coffee, and inquired what she had heard of General Rodes. She told me his body had been saved and sent to Lynchburg. Many of my wounded comrades wept aloud and bitterly on learning for the first time the fate of their beloved commander. All seemed overcome with unaffected grief. General Goodwin of North Carolina, and Col. G. W. Patton were killed, and General York of Louisiana, lost an arm. The brave Capt. Tom Lightfoot of the 6th Alabama, by whose side I have stood in many a battle, was instantly killed. He was a younger brother of Col. J. N. Lightfoot. The enemy lost Brigadier General Russell killed, and Generals Upton, Mcintosh and Chapman wounded. Report says that over 6,000 Yankee wounded are now scattered over Winchester in every available building. Private houses have been seized and turned into hospitals, and their inmates forced to seek other quarters. The churches, too, are used. It has been a victory bought at a fearful cost to them, if it be a victory at all.

Surgeons Cromwell and Love, of North Carolina, and Surgeons T. J. Weatherly, of the 6th Alabama, and Robert Hardy, of the 3rd Alabama, were left in charge of our wounded. Captain Hewlett and I were moved to a well ventilated room on the second floor and placed on a comfortable mattress. A short time after an elegant lady came in to see us, and inquired from what State we hailed. I replied, "Alabama," whereupon she said she had lost a favorite cousin, a captain in an Alabama regiment, killed at Seven Pines. He proved to be Captain Keeling of my company, and the good woman, Mrs. Mary Greenhow Lee (now of Baltimore), proposed to take us under her special care, and to have us carried to a private house where we would be better provided for. We gladly consented, and, after a brief absence, she returned with some litters, borne by negroes, who still remained faithful to their owners, despite the corrupting influence of the Yankees, and were carried to the law office once used by Hon. James M. Mason, our Minister to England, and his able partner, Mr. Clark. The office was on Main street, near Fort Hill, so-called from the remains of an old fort erected there in the days of the British General Braddock, and near the residence of Mr. Clark and his amiable daughter, Mrs. Susan P. Jones. Mrs. Jones sent us some delicacies, and made us a brief visit. I suffered much from my wound today. A party of Confederates, perhaps a hundred, marched by the office, under guard, on their way to some Northern prison. The sight was a painful one.

Major Lambeth, Lieutenant W H. Hearne, Sergeant Lines and private Watkins, of the 14th North Carolina, were brought to the office and quartered with us. Captain Frost, of the 4th Georgia, from West Point, Ga., died of his wounds in hospital. The ladies gave him the kindest attention.

Yankees are continually passing our door, and frequently stop and gaze curiously and impertinently at us, and ask rude, 'tantalizing questions. They do not wait to be invited in, but stalk in noisily and roughly. Their conversation is coarse and insulting.

We have many conflicting and unreliable rumors of Early's movements. Six families, in the vicinity of the office, have agreed to alternately furnish us with our daily meals. They are those of Mrs. Susan Peyton Jones, Mrs. J. N. Swartzwelder, Mrs. Burwell, Mrs. W. G. Kiger, Mrs. Snapp and Mrs. Marsteller. Three times each day they send us very palatable and abundant meals, nicely cooked, and of fine variety. Negro slaves bring them to us, and are very attentive and respectful, sincerely sympathizing with us in our sufferings, and openly declaring their purpose to remain with their mistresses (their masters are absent in the Southern army), and not regard the seductive promises made by the Yankees to induce them to abandon their life-long friends and homes.

Several pretty girls called to see us, and entertained us very agreeably with their charming conversation. Among them were Misses Nena Kiger, Gertrude Coffroth, Sallie Hoffman, Jennie Taylor, and Lizzie Swartzwelder. They are true to the cause and encourage us much.

September 25. (Sunday). All the churches in the city, except one, are filled with Yankee wounded. Our surgeons say our wounded will not number over 500, while theirs is between 4,000 and 5,000, nearly ten times greater than ours. Their killed is said to be equal to our killed and wounded together. Verily, a costly victory for them!

Miss Janet Fauntleroy, a very pretty and intelligent young lady, came to the office and brought us some delicacies. She is a granddaughter of Brigadier General Fauntleroy, perhaps the oldest officer on the rolls of the Confederate army, now over eighty years of age, and daughter of Captain Fauntleroy of the Confederate navy, now serving his country on the high seas, aiding Admiral Semmes, Captain Maffitt, Commodore Maury and other gallant seamen. My wound gives me constant pain. The torn flesh protrudes nearly two inches, and the severed nerves torture me much.

September 27th, 28th and 29th. Three days of great suffering. Small bones are constantly working their way out of my wound, and the separated nerves and sinews keep me awake, night and day. The good ladies are ministering angels, so incessant are they in their kind attentions. They are doing most excellent service in the Confederate hospital, greatly assisting the surgeons. We owe them a debt of lasting gratitude.

One afternoon, while in conversation with the beautiful Miss Nena Kiger, a sharp piece of bone, making its exit from my wound, cut an artery, and "secondary hemorrhage" was produced. Miss Nena ran immediately for a surgeon, and, in an incredibly short time, returned with Dr. Hardy, who promptly applied sulphate of iron and bandaged my leg very tightly from the foot to the knee, thus checking the dangerous hemorrhage. The blood flowed in jets from the artery, and I soon became very faint and deathly sick. Drs. Weatherly and Hardy came to see me frequently during the day and night, and, although they gave me two large doses of morphine, I could not sleep at all for the pain. Poor John Attaway died of his wound at the residence of Mrs. Hist. He spoke often, while in his right mind, and in his delirium, affectionately of his mother, of Sergeant Stafford and myself. Mrs. Hist brought me some parting message from him. May his brave spirit rest in peace!

The severed nerves in my left foot, below my wound, caused me real agony. My comrades in the office are cheerful and seem to improve. Sergeant Lines of the 14th North Carolina, is a native of the North, but is a true Southerner in sentiment. Some of our best soldiers were born in the North, and deserve honor for their devotion to truth and their adopted homes.

Rumors are rife that General Early will attempt to retake Winchester soon. This is very improbable, as Sheridan's forces are too numerous. Reinforcements pass by the office every day going to the front, and Early's army must be a mere handful of exhausted, illy equipped men, incapable of any offensive movement. The ladies bring us all kinds of reports, usually very cheering. They always look on the bright side. Mosby's men venture into the city quite often at night, to see relatives and friends, and gain all the information they can. They are greeted warmly, and secreted by the citizens until they are ready to leave the city. They carry out many letters for Dixie Land. The risk they run is very great, but they are daring scouts, accustomed to danger and fond of its excitement.

The Twelfth's Artillery Associations.

This sketch would be incomplete if I did not mention the gallant batteries which were associated with our regiment and brigade from the beginning to the close of the war, and to which we became greatly attached. Captain Thomas H. Carter, afterwards colonel of a battalion of artillery, commanded Carter's battery in the first part of the war, and was a gifted and gallant soldier. Since the war he has become very prominent in railroad circles, but has retired to his country home in King William County, Va. His accomplished brother, Captain William Page Carter, succeeded him in command of the battery, and won renown by his intrepid and patriotic conduct in field and camp. He is now a well known author, living at Boyce, Va., and has published a volume of poems called *Echoes of the Glen*.

Soon after the battle of Seven Pines Captain Carter wrote a stirring poem, commemorative of that great battle, which I think is worthy of repetition in this connection, especially as he alludes in complimentary terms to the 12th Alabama regiment:

"Rodes' Brigade at Seven Pines, May 31st, 1862.

"Down by the valley 'mid thunder and lightning,
Down by the valley mid jettings of light, Down by the deep crimson valley of Richmond,
The twenty-five hundred moved on to the fight. Onward, still onward, to the portals of glory,
To the sepulchered chambers, yet never dismayed, Down by the deep crimson valley of Richmond,
Marched the bold warriors of Rodes' brigade.
"See ye the fires and flashes still leaping,
Hear ye the beating and pelting of storm, See ye the banners of proud Alabama,
In front of her columns move steadily on; Hear ye the music that gladdens each comrade
As it comes through the air 'mid torrents of sounds, Hear ye the booming adown the red valley,
Carter unbuckles his swarthy old hounds.
"Twelfth Mississippi! I saw your brave column
Push through the channels of living and dead,
Twelfth Alabama! why weep your old war horse,*

He died, as he wished, in the gear at, your head. Seven Pines! you will tell on the pages of glory,

How the blood of the South ebbed away 'neath your shade , How the lads of Virginia fought in the Red Valley

And fell in the column of Rodes' brigade.

"Fathers and mothers, ye weep for your jewels, Sisters, ye weep for your brothers in vain,

Maidens, ye weep for your sunny-eyed lovers, Weep, for they never can come back again.

* Col. R. T. Jones.

Weep ye, but know that the signet of freedom Is stamped in the hillocks of earth newly made,

And know ye that victory, the shrine of the mighty, Stands forth on the colors of Rodes' brigade.

"Maidens of Southland! come bring ye bright flowers,

Weave ye a chaplet for the brow of the brave, Bring ye the emblems of Freedom and Victory,

Bring ye the emblems of Death and the Grave, Bring ye some motto befitting a Hero,

Bring ye exotics that never will fade, Come to the deep crimsoned valley of Richmond

And crown the young chieftain who led his brigade."*

*Major General R. E.Rodes

Preaching in Camp.

The 12th Alabama was singularly fortunate in having two such superior Chaplains as Rev. Mark S. Andrews, D. D., of the Alabama Conference, and Rev. Henry D. Moore, D. D., of the South Carolina Conference, at Opelika. These were able men, fine preachers, and earnest and faithful in their labors. Dr. Moore was assisted in his labors, during the latter part of the war, by the ministrations of Rev. William A. Moore, of Company F, now living at Neches, Texas. Moore was a college classmate of mine, a first rate speaker, fluent, earnest and modest. He ought to have been made the chaplain of the regiment at one time, but served his country in the ranks, having been transferred, as he flatteringly told me, from the 60th Georgia to my company, because I was a commissioned officer in it, and on account of his kind regard for me. He was one of the members of my company that was present at the surrender of General Lee at Appomattox, and since the war has been a citizen of Texas.

Rev. E. J. Rogers, a Baptist minister, also of our company, who came as a substitute, was a good preacher. He had the misfortune to lose his leg at the battle of Gettysburg, and, as I was wounded there, and in the hospital tent, near him, I remember distinctly his earnest, pleading prayers while suffering and submitting to the amputation of his leg. He was a man gifted in prayer and was a gallant soldier. I have never heard what became of him.

In the early part of the war our company and brigade were favored with sermons from some distinguished Richmond ministers.

Major-General R. E. Rodes.

Among these I recall Rev. Wm. Brown, D. D., a Presbyterian, Rev. J. L. Burrows, D. D., a Baptist minister, and it is worthy of record that this man of God was with the wounded of the Twelfth Alabama on the night of the 31st of May, 1862, at Seven Pines, and during the entire night he was busy ministering to the dead and dying, seeing that the wounded were placed in ambulances and carried to the Richmond hospitals. I can recall his passing by our regiment and near my company on the first of June of that year, following an ambulance which contained the wounded body of my friend and messmate, Mack Flournoy, of Opelika, one of my sergeants. In the rear of the ambulance walked Flourney's slave and cook, Mark, a negro well-known to every man in the regiment, and universally liked As poor Mark passed by Company F with his head bowed, he looked over to the members of the company and burst into tears, and in tender tones called out, "I have lost my best friend, Marse Mack is in the ambulance and I don't believe he will ever get well." He was right in his prophecy, for M. A. Flournoy, my intelligent, gallant friend, died a week later.

Rev. L. Rosser, D. D., of Winchester, also preached to us more than once, and showed himself to be a great orator.

Rev. Dr. W. C. Powell, now of the North Carolina Conference, made frequent visits to the Twelfth Alabama, and gave us good sermons.

We were seldom able to attend divine service in churches, and usually lay upon the ground, in groups, near the minister, while he delivered his discourse to us. The meetings of our brigade Christian Association, as well as the one of the Twelfth Alabama, were usually well attended. The only requirements of the latter were that we should not indulge in drinking intoxicating liquors nor in profanity, and some of the wickedest men in the camp joined it, and I am glad to report, refrained from the use of profanity afterwards. Among these were two prominent officers, whose names I will not give.

While in camp, near the Rappahannock river, Chaplain Moore induced several of the officers to deliver Sunday night lectures, and I remember well a very fine one given by Captain John J. Nicholson, of Company I. Captain Nicholson was a gallant officer, a graduate of St. John's College, Md., and a teacher at Spring Hill College, Mobile. He was the bravest man in battle, to be a braggart, that I ever saw. He never flinched from danger, and more than once took the battle flag of the regiment from the color bearer, waved it aloft, and rushed in front of the command, but he didn't fail to boast about it next day

Dr. Moore complimented me by selecting me to deliver one number in his course of lectures, and I had busied myself writing a speech on "True Courage," but the Sunday night I was to deliver it found us marching, and it was never heard.

General Battle and Major R. H. Powell, of the Third Alabama, from Union Springs, were prominent members of our Christian Association. The disposition of a large majority of the men was religious, and I fully believe that the vast majority of those whose lives were lost had their noble souls translated to the realms of the hereafter, to live forever with the good and true.

Music in the Camp.

Our Confederate soldiers had their hours of rest and relaxation, and sometimes music of various kinds was interspersed with their recreation hours. There were a few fiddlers in the 12th Alabama, but the most noted and skillful one was Ben Smith of my company, an old bachelor, a quiet but true soldier, always ready for duty. He was a Georgian, like myself, in an Alabama regiment. His skill with the fiddle was unequaled. I have heard many violinists since the war, in the great orchestras of Thomas and Sousa and Creatore, but none of their number could equal great Ben Smith. He had gifts, and his knowledge of distinctive Southern music, peculiar to country life, some of which I have heard our slaves often play with exquisite taste and great gusto on our Georgia plantations, was wonderful. Among the choicest in Smith's repertoire were, *Hell broke loose in Georgia, Billy in the Low Grounds, Arkansas Traveller, Dixie, Money Musk, The Goose Hangs High, When I saw Sweet Nellie Home, My Old Kentucky Home, When This Cruel War is Over, The Girl I Left Behind Me,* etc. Crowds would gather around him and laugh and applaud and clap their hands, and joyously express their pleasure and appreciation.

Then sometimes sweet songs would float through the air from manly voices, and *Backward, Turn Backward, Oh Time in Your Flight, All Quiet Along the Potomac To-night, Dixie, Lorena, Marseillaise,* etc., were among the songs sung. Occasionally, particularly on Sunday, we would have hymns, and the songs at church were sung with great sweetness and reverence.

When encamped on the banks of the Rapidan, and on the Rappahannock, often we could hear snatches of songs from the encampment or pickets of the Federal soldiers on the opposite side of the river, and our men, satisfied that there was no danger from the hands of the enemy, would sing from our side, and more than once the sweet tones of *Home, Sweet Home,* were sung by the opposing men, and echoed and re-echoed from bank to bank. This rare, unequaled song of John Howard Payne always recalled the tenderest recollections, and sweetest memories, and banished every evil thought.

The Twelfth Alabama Surgeons.

This regiment was fortunate in having skilled and faithful surgeons. The first when we entered service were Dr. Geo. Whitfield of Old Spring Hill, Alabama, as surgeon, but who became later brigade surgeon, and was assisted by Dr. Edward A. Ligon of Tuskegee, brother of Hon. R. F Ligon, first Captain of Co. F. He died soon after returning home, in the winter of 1861 and 1862, after his resignation. Dr. Whitfield is still living in Marengo county, having happily married a noble lady of Richmond. He is past his threescore years and ten, is in splendid health, full of energy and often rides twenty miles a day on horseback, relieving the sick in his county. He was one of the most accomplished of surgeons and physicians, and greatly beloved.

Wm. Wallace Scott, formerly of Mississippi, was also at one time our assistant surgeon. The other assistant surgeon of this regiment, who served for a short time during the war was, Dr. John B. Kelly of Anniston. He enlisted as a private in Co. B, and was promoted assistant surgeon.

Battle of the Wilderness.

The succession of fierce engagements, known as the battles of the Wilderness, which began May 5th, 1864, and continued through May 12th, were events of surpassing interest to the Confederate States. The meeting on the 5th of May between parts of General Lee's army and that of General Grant, was not a great distance from the old Chancellorsville battle ground. Rodes' brigade fought in the woods most of the time, and the writer had the bad luck to have a minie ball, which had struck the limb of a tree, to glance and pierce the ankle of his right foot, cutting through the shoe, skin and flesh and grazing the bone, but did not retire from the field. Here gallant Ed. Hendree, while leading the sharpshooters, was struck by a fatal bullet. No purer, braver young officer followed the fortunes of Lee. The late afternoon of the 5th was devoted, from sundown until 10 o'clock, in throwing up some hasty breastworks. At that hour I crept over the works with two canteens of water for the purpose of relieving some of the wounded enemy, who were groaning and calling aloud in our front. The night was dark, with no moon and very few .stars visible, and as I crawled to the first man and offered him a drink of water, he declined, and in reply to my inquiries, told me that he had been shot through the leg and the body, and was sure that he was bleeding internally. I told him that I feared he would not live until morning, and asked him whether he was making any preparation for leaving this world. His reply was that he had not been given it any thought, as his life had not been one of sin, and that he was content. He was about twenty years of age and from a northwestern State. I continued my search among the men, many of whom I found too far gone to reply to my questions, and others quietly drank the proffered water and thanked me for the attention. I occupied myself in this way for some time, and approached very near to the pickets and the main line of the enemy. The light of the next day enabled us to see many dead men in our front, but no visible living enemy.

On the 8th we were again under heavy fire, and on the 10th a fierce engagement took place, and we were running backwards and forwards for hours; first advancing and then retreating.

At night I had the roll called and only one man failed to answer. That was brave John Attaway. About midnight he appeared, came to the tree where I was lying, and explained, in reply to my stern inquiry as to where he had been, that he had got lost from the company and gone into the fight with a South Carolina regiment, and that he had the permission of the colonel to refer to him for the truth of his statement. He handed me the sword of the colonel of a Massachusetts regiment, as well as his splendid blue broadcloth coat, with all of the insignia of a colonel's rank upon it. These were given to me by him in the hope, I presume, of conciliating me and excusing his absence. The coat, sword and belt I sent to Major Vandiver, in charge of the Alabama depot in Richmond, and never heard from them again. They were no doubt captured when Richmond fell.

The Twelfth of May

This was a day of trial, danger and desperation. The great battle of the triangle took place. I saw General Gordon and his A. D. C., Lieutenant Hutchinson, ride on top of the breastworks in our front, hats off and drawn swords, calling to the men not to fire in their front, as they were shooting into Doles' Georgia brigade which had driven the enemy from our front. This daring and gallant action won the admiration and applause of the brigade, and caused every man to cease firing.

In one of our rearward movements we stopped at an inner line of rude works, and General Battle established his headquarters with my company. While sitting and standing, awaiting directions, a number of Yankee foreigners, without arms or accouterments, jumped over our breastworks, and in foreign jargon, begged for quarter. They were evidently full of whiskey or other stimulant. They were ordered to run to the rear, and lost no time in obeying.

While at this point Major Whiting rode up and delivered a message to General Battle directing a rapid advance over the breastworks and to the front. To this order the general demurred, laying that his men had been fighting so continuously, and were so utterly exhausted, that he felt confident that it would be impossible to preserve any alignment, and that he did not believe a forward movement wise or practicable. Whiting's reply was, "I will report to General Rodes," but in a few minutes he galloped back and repeated his command, and in response, General Battle ordered his brigade to "forward." For a long distance we were under constant firing, and had little opportunity to reply. A number of men were shot down as we advanced, but the regiment and brigade maintained its line and continued moving slowly onward. After dark we were halted in a woods not a great distance from the Federal troops, and fronting them, were directed not to sit nor lie down, but to be ready for any movement. Colonel Goodgame came to me, as I stood at the head of the company and regiment, and said that he felt it absolutely necessary for him to have a few minutes sleep, and proposed that while he hugged an oak sapling that I remain awake and receive any orders that might come, and arouse him, adding that when he had slept a few minutes he would relieve me and I could sleep against the sapling. In this way we spent some time, how long it is impossible for me to relate. It was a night of unrest, of misery, of horror. The standing men would occasionally hear a comrade utter an exclamation as a stray bullet from the enemy pierced some part of his body and placed him *hors du combat*. And it was well that the men were kept standing, as I saw many of them walking first by the right flank and then by the left flank, and in profound sleep, wholly unconscious of what they were doing. These were hours that tried men's souls.

The next day Grant's forces had disappeared from our front, and we were told that they were marching towards Hanover C. H. in an effort to flank General Lee and get between him and Richmond. I walked over the famous salient, so much discussed by critics and historians, where General Edward Johnson and some of his troops were captured, and I saw the stump of a hickory tree, probably six inches in diameter, which is now in the museum of the Smithsonian Institute at Washington. The stump had been literally cut in two by the myriads of bullets that had pierced it, and the top of the tree was lying prone beside the stump. What chance would there have been for soldiers lying in front or in rear of this tree? Limbs, leaves, and bodies of small trees were lying thick in this part of the battlefield. One gallant fellow remarked, that, in all his experience during the war, he believed that this was the "hottest place" that he had ever seen.

It was during these fights that General Lee, anxious to restore order and to drive the enemy from a certain position, rode on Traveler to the head of a regiment and called to the men to follow him in a charge upon the enemy. General Gordon was not far distant, and riding up to General Lee, urged him to retire, that his life was too precious to be placed in such jeopardy, and that he himself would lead the men. Two soldiers took the reins of Traveler, and despite General Lee's remonstrances, but amid the earnest exclamations of approval, led the horse and General Lee to the rear, while General Gordon led his men gallantly forward and drove the enemy before him, relieving the situation.

After the 13th for several days the two great leaders maneuvered for advantage, Grant continuing his flank movement while Lee kept in front of him, offering daily battle. These movements continued until the two armies reached Richmond, and soon thereafter General Early was detached and sent on his famous campaign through the Valley and to Washington, which has been described elsewhere in this sketch.

General R. E. Rodes

A fine martial poem, called, *"The Man of the Twelfth of May,"* written by Captain Robert Falligant, of Savannah, fitly and eloquently describes this remarkable and heroic incident. From it I make the following extract:

> "When history tells her story,
> Of the noble hero band,
> Who made the green fields gory
> For the life of their native land,
> How grand will be the picture
> Of Georgia's proud array
> As they drove the boasting foemen back
> On that glorious Twelfth of May !
> Whose mien is ever proudest
> When we hold the foe at bay ?
> Whose war-cry cheers us loudest
> As we rush to the bloody fray ?
> 'Tis Gordon's — our reliance,
> Fearless as on that day
> When he hurled his grand defiance
> In that charge of the Twelfth of May.
> Who, who can be a coward ?
> What freeman fear to die
> When Gordon orders 'forward!'
> And the red cross floats on high ?
> Follow his tones inspiring,
> On, on to the field! Away !
> And we see the foe retiring
> As it did on the Twelfth of May !"

www.ingramcontent.com/pod-product-compliance
Lightning Source LLC
Chambersburg PA
CBHW050513240426
43673CB00004B/205